PIVOTAL MOMENTS IN GOD'S STORY

TURNING POINTS

STEVEN LLOYD

CLOSER LOOK BOOKS

Also by Steven Lloyd

Coping: A Biblical Approach (2004)

For my grandchildren:
Kylie
Danielle
Hope
Collin
Joel
Jacob

CONTENTS

ACKNOWLEDGMENTS

I am thankful for the help given by so many for the completion of this book: Michael Benfield, Clint Brown, Jennifer Vaughn-Estrada, Jim Lloyd, Randy Mabe, Don Ruhl, Corey Schissler, Sandy Souza, Don Walker, Randy Watson, James Weakland, and Michael Whitworth.

I want to thank Josh Feit at www.evangela.com for designing the cover.

I also want to thank my elders for allowing me to present this material in an extended series of sermons at the church in Chino, CA: Reuben Lacuata, Gene Rupel, and Corey Schissler.

Unless otherwise stated, biblical quotations are taken from the English Standard Version of the Bible, copyright 2004 by Crossway Bibles.

NOTE: My use of the word "story" in the book is of concern to some. I do not mean by it the same thing that is meant by the word "fiction." A story can be a report of actual historical events told in an artistic fashion. The Scriptures tell us the truth about the history of the world. The writers recount that history in an artistic fashion. That is what makes it literature as well as history. The author of Ecclesiastes expresses this literary approach to writing: "The Preacher sought to find words of delight, and uprightly he wrote words of truth" (12:10).

INTRODUCTION

I received my first Bible as a gift from my grandmother on December 25, 1962. I was nine years old. I was moved by her gift, but only because I knew through movies and television that it was supposed to be a special book. Cecil B. DeMille, the director of several epoch movies, was the only teller of Bible stories I knew. Charlton Heston, the actor who played Moses in "The Ten Commandments," was the only holy man. Beyond that, I was not sure what to make of it. It was a talisman, a lucky charm.

Our family was not a religious one. No appeals were ever made to the Bible, or to God, to support any belief or decision, or to reinforce any kind of moral behavior. The only time Bible-related topics were discussed was when I, or one of my siblings, asked questions like: "Mom, what are we religiously?" or, "Do you believe in God?" or "Is Jesus the Son of God?"

I remember picking up my gift-Bible on a number of occasions wondering what to do with it, wondering where to begin, wondering how to begin. I was a poor reader. I struggled with comprehension, and quickly gave up trying. So, the Bible remained an unresolved Rubik's Cube.

Enter Valerie. We met in junior high school, and began dating in high school. I eventually attended church with her and embraced the gospel on June 27, 1971. Some of what the Bible taught came into clearer focus. I could even remember a text here and there. Eventually, I was invited to teach a high school Bible class.

My hunger for knowing God and understanding Scripture grew along with my desire to leave my job with the phone company to attend a school of biblical studies. I attended the Southern California School of Evangelism (SCSE) in Buena Park, California. We studied the Bible book-by-book, church history, logic, English, and whatever else the leadership deemed important. The course that came closest to helping me see the Bible as a whole was taught by Don Sullivan. The course was the Scheme of Redemption, a subject he studied under Ed Wharton. Don helped us to see the thread that held all sixty-six books together. It began with the promise God gave to Abraham—that in his seed all the nations of the earth would be blessed—and how that promise was fulfilled in Jesus Christ. My appreciation for the story dimension that provides the literary vehicle for redemption history came a dozen years later.

Leland Ryken begins his book, *Words of Delight*, writing:

Because the Bible is a book with religious authority we tend to assume that it is a theology book. But if we look at how the Bible presents its material it resembles a literary work more than anything else. It is filled with stories, poems, visions, and letters. The thing that it is emphatically not is what we so often picture it as being—a theological outline with proof texts attached. (11, 1993)

The Bible tells a story. It is God's story. It is about God's mission, the Story of redemption. It tells us how God saves man through His Son to God's glory. Paul states it succinctly in the long rich sentence that opens the letter to the Ephesians (1:3-14). Three times he affirms that man's salvation is to the praise of the glory of God's grace (Eph. 1:6, 12, 14). He summarizes the theme of the Bible when he writes that God, "through Christ reconciled us to himself" (2 Cor. 5:18). John summarizes the story with the words of a great multitude crying out with a loud voice, "Salvation belongs to our God who sits on the throne, and to the Lamb!" (Rev. 7:10)

The aim of this work is to point the reader to the underlying Story of the Bible. That Story is the thread connecting Genesis to Revelation and every book in between. It provides the context for the individual doctrines by which we do business. It will help the reader to understand their origin, purpose, and destination because the story the Bible tells is also our story. It will tell us how the world got into the mess it is in, and how to get out of it. These are the sorts of things that form worldviews.

OUTLINE OF THE BOOK

Every story has a beginning, middle, and an end. The beginning of the Story the Bible tells is easy to find. It is in the opening pages of the first book—Genesis. We find the middle of the Story at the cross of Jesus Christ, and the Story ends with His return.

There are hundreds of episodes that make up the whole Story. Some of those episodes move the Story along to a greater degree than others. There are around a dozen such episodes. These *turning points* alter the direction of the Story, or advance it in some way.

Other books have been written that help readers to understand the Bible book-by-book. This book will draw primarily from the narrative sections of the Bible (Genesis to 2 Chronicles; the Gospel accounts, and Acts), and from the more expositional (the prophets and the letters of the New Testament), and poetic (the Psalms) texts to supplement what is written in story form.

To get us started, I would like to simplify matters by pointing you to some work done by N. T. Wright (Wright, p. 141 NTPG, 1992). Professor Wright suggests that the Story of the Bible can be divided into five acts:

Act 1 Creation

Act 2 The Fall

Act 3 Israel

Act 4 Jesus

Act 5 The Church

Craig Bartholomew adds a sixth act to N. T. Wright's five-act scenario. He adds the story of "The Return of Christ." We will follow suit by calling the sixth act, "The Return of the King" (13, 2004).

Other students of the Bible view the Story a bit differently, in particular the last two acts. I am not going to spend time refuting paradigms I think are off the mark, or defending the Story as I present it in this book. My primary purpose is to help the reader understand that the connecting thread of the entire Bible is best seen by means of the cohesive story it tells. If you do not know the Story, perhaps this is a good place to begin. Later, if you disagree with the outline I provide, you will know why you disagree. At least you will have begun to see the Bible through a narrative lens.

While my breakdown of the Story takes into account six acts, my focus will be on the major *turning points* in the Story. The subtitle of this book is: *Pivotal Moments in God's Story*. The emphasis is on *Turning Points*. While five of the six Acts are *turning points* in themselves, Act 3 contains six turning points.

The *turning points* are as follows:

1. The Beginning
2. The Fall
3. The Promise
4. The Giving of the Law
5. Give Us a King (two chapters)
6. The Departure of God
7. The Return Home
8. Hanukkah
9. The Resurrection
10. The Church
11. The Return of the King

The concluding chapter identifies several of the benefits that accompany knowing this Story.

CHAPTER ONE

THE CREATION

We have passed through what some call the "post-modern" era. Jean-Francois Lyotard argued that the most distinctive feature of Postmodernism is its denial of a "grand narrative" or meta-narrative, meaning there is no undergirding story that holds all of human history together.

While Mr. Lyotard's observation may be spot on, the Postmodern notion that there is no grand narrative is false. The Bible gives us one. Its grand unifying Story is what this book is all about.

Like every other well-structured story, the Bible has a beginning, middle, and an end. The Story of the Bible begins with the creation of all things. The middle of the Story is located in the Gospel accounts, and centers on the life and work of Jesus the Messiah with emphasis on His death, burial, resurrection, appearances, and ascension. The end of the Story will come when Jesus delivers the kingdom to God, the Father: when He abolishes all rule, and all authority, and power (1 Corinthians 15:24).

This chapter begins with—well, the beginning, and ends with a look at the implications of creation, and a consideration of how we ought to respond.

A SUBLIME BEGINNING

Some books have distinguished themselves, in part, by memorable opening lines. I do not think I will ever forget how J. R. R. Tolkien's story, *The Hobbit*, begins:

> In a hole in the ground there lived a hobbit. Not a nasty, dirty, wet hole, filled with the ends of worms and an oozy smell, nor yet a dry, bare, sandy hole with nothing in it to sit down on or to eat: it was a hobbit-hole, and that means comfort.

Who has read—and can forget—the whimsical opening line

of Jane Austen's *Pride and Prejudice?*

> It is a truth universally acknowledged, that a single man in possession
> of a good fortune, must be in want of a wife.

The opening lines of Dante's *Divine Comedy* are chilling:

> Midway in the journey of our life
> I came to myself in a dark wood,
> for the straight way was lost.
> Ah, how hard it is to tell
> the nature of that wood, savage, dense and harsh—
> the very thought of it renews my fear!
> How I came there I cannot really tell,
> I was so full of sleep
> when I forsook the one true way.

I do not know if I can put my finger on the reason why, but
the profoundly simple opening line of Job is memorable:

> There was a man in the land of Uz whose name was Job.

The first line in Genesis, the first book in the Bible, deserves
first place among memorable first lines in literature:

> In the beginning God created the heavens and the earth (Genesis 1:1).

Longinus, a first century literary critic, refers to the first
chapter of Genesis to define what he meant by the word
"sublime" (meaning "lofty" or "elevated") when applied to
literature.

…the legislator of the Jews, no ordinary man, having formed and expressed a worthy conception of the might of the Godhead, writes at the very beginning of his laws, "God said,"—what? "Let there be light, and there was light; let there be land, and there was land." (Adams 99).

Terry Pratchett is a British author who fuses fantasy with satire. He begins the book *Hogfather,* one of his popular Discworld books, by writing:

Everything starts somewhere, although many physicists disagree. But people have always been dimly aware of the problem with the start of things. They wonder aloud how the snowplow driver gets to work, or how the makers of dictionaries look up the spellings of the words. Yet there is the constant desire to find some point in the twisting, knotting, raveling nets of space-time on which a metaphorical finger can be put to indicate that here, *here*, is the point where it all began…

People want to know how things came to be.[1]

The History Channel produced a multi-part drama called *Vikings.* In one episode, a raiding party of Vikings sailed West to England. They killed all but a few of the monks in a monastery and brought the few remaining priests home to sell as slaves.

---

[1] To the contrary, Daniel Boorstin, the late Librarian of Congress, argues that the sacred hymns of the Hindu religion are so preoccupied with the "shining ones," which is what they call the gods, that they were not at all interested in origins. He writes, "How the world once came into being or how it might end seemed irrelevant before the brightness of the visible world" (Boorstin, p. 4). It is difficult for me, with my Christian and Western World mindset, to relate to the Hindu mindset on this subject.

The head of the raiding party, Ragnar, kept one priest as a slave for himself and his family.

In one scene, the priest curiously asks the Vikings how the earth was made. They tell him that a giant creature named Ymir was killed by Odin and his brothers, and from Ymir's body, the earth was made. His blood was transformed into oceans and water. His flesh became the land; bones became the mountains, teeth formed rocks; his hair became the grass and trees. They threw his brains up in the air and it became the clouds, and the skull became the dome we call sky.

They then turned to the Monk, "So, how do you think it was made, priest?" End of scene. Commercial.

THREE IMPORTANT WORDS

The opening line of the Bible contains three important words: "beginning," "God," and "created."

The Bible affirms there was a *beginning*. Some, like the physicists referred to in Terry Pratchett's book, want to affirm that there was no beginning, that the material universe has always existed. Whether one accepts the explanation proposed by Moses at this point in our study is irrelevant. What is important now is knowing how the writers of the Bible portray the origin of all things. For Moses, there was a beginning.

The second important word is *God*. Prior to the beginning, or the origin of all things, there was God. God predates creation. His very Being is what philosophers call "necessary" —meaning that His existence, His eternal existence, is necessary to the being or existence of everything else. And the power of *being* is His alone. The Apostle Paul, before the disciples of Socrates, affirmed, "In Him we live, and move and have our very being" (Acts 17:28).

The third important word is *created*. The story of creation is unique among creation accounts found in other cultures. For example, some traditions affirm that matter is eternal and that God simply took the raw materials that have always existed and formed them to His liking, as in the story the Vikings told. Others say that everything that exists is divine, meaning that everything that exists is god. This is the doctrine called pantheism; "pan" meaning *all*, and "theism" meaning *God*. This, naturally, leads to worshiping nature.

The Creation points us to its Maker, but Creation should not be confused with being the Maker. He existed prior to, and independent of the things He created. The heavens are not God, but they declare the glory of God (Psalm 19:1).

Other texts reflect on the ideas initially expressed in the opening line of Scripture. See, for example, Proverbs 8:22-31 and Psalm 33.

After the summary-like statement of Genesis 1:1, Moses fleshes out the story. There is a word-pattern: "God said... And there was... And there was evening and there was morning..." On days three and six, He even said, "And God saw that it was good" (Genesis 1:10, 25). There is a break in the pattern of God's assessment of creation on the sixth day. The Lord said, "It is not good that the man should be alone" (Genesis 2:18). So, from Adam's side God formed Eve. Genesis One ends: "And God saw everything that he had made and behold, it was very good" (Genesis 1:31).

When considering the biblical narrative about origins, it is important that we hear the author spell things out in his own terms without trying to tweak or reconstruct it. It is when we come to the end of the narrative of the Bible that more sense is made of the beginning.

The Story of the Bible begins with the loss of innocence, the introduction of guilt, a loss of access to immortality, a loss of Eden, and separation from God. For God's family, the Story of the Bible ends with access to a river of the water of life, and to the tree of life (lost in the beginning); forgiveness, and life in the presence of God (Revelation 22:1-5). The closing chapters of the Bible tell us that we gain the very things humanity lost in the beginning of the story. The end makes sense of the beginning. The beginning finds its significance or fulfillment in the end.

Some have tried making sense of the beginning in light of scientific theories—the "how"—of creation, rather than making sense out of it in light of the narrative in which it is found. My encouragement to the reader is to begin by considering the account in light of the Story as a whole.

IMPLICATIONS OF CREATION

What does the doctrine of creation imply? One thing it implies is that God is infinite in wisdom.

> O LORD, how manifold are your works!
> In wisdom have you made them all;
> the earth is full of your creations (Psalm 104:24).

The Old Testament prophet Isaiah writes,

Have you not known? Have you not heard?
The LORD is the everlasting God,
  the Creator of the ends of the earth.
He does not faint nor grow weary;
  his understanding is unsearchable (Isaiah 40:28).

God's creation also implies infinite power. Can you imagine the kind of power required to bring something into existence from nothing—by the sheer force of will? This is the power of being itself. The apostle Paul argues that God's power and divine nature are clearly manifested in the things He created (Romans 1:20). "The universe is a masterpiece of wisdom and order" (Piper, p. 91).

John Goldingay writes,

Create is a gripping verb in this gripping first line… Only God 'creates.' Creating involves exercising an extraordinary, effortless sovereignty in order to bring something into being. The verb draws attention to the amazing nature of what God does, bringing something into being against all the odds" (6).

WHY DID GOD CREATE?

When I began taking the work of evangelism seriously in the mid 1970's, I found myself at the kitchen table of a high school student and his sister. I was not that much older than our young hosts. Our discussion was interrupted with a question from their mother who happened to be hovering around the outskirts of our discussion. She asked if she could pose a question. We gladly opened the discussion to entertain her question. She asked, "Why did God create anything at all?"

I had never thought to ask the question myself. All I could say was, "Good question," but I didn't have an answer for her. I knew the Scriptures affirmed *that* God created the universe by speaking it all into existence, but I did not know *why*. My ears have been open ever since, waiting for an answer to that great question.

We have been left some clues. Consider the words of the heavenly choir,

> Worthy are you, our Lord and God to receive glory and honor and power, for you created all things and by your will they existed and were created" (Revelation 4:11)

Perhaps this is our first clue. God created of His own will. He did not create of necessity or by coercion from any outside source.

Second, several times in Genesis One God creates something or someone and He concludes by saying, "and it was good." So, everything God created was good. It pleased Him.

Third, the heavens were created to declare God's glory (Psalm 19:1). This may very well help us to understand why He created man.

I think it is safe to conclude that the reason God created anything at all was to display His glory out of His good pleasure.

HOW SHOULD WE RESPOND?

Let's see how others have responded to these wonderful realities.

Let all the earth fear the LORD;
let all the inhabitants of the world stand in awe of Him! (Psalm 33:8).

Psalm 104 rehearses a number of ways that God's power manifests itself as He provides for and rules over His creation. Psalm 104:31-34.

> May the glory of the LORD endure forever;
> may the LORD rejoice in his works,
> who looks on the earth and it trembles,
> who touches the mountains and they smoke!
> I will sing to the LORD as long as I live;
> I will sing praise to my God while I have being.
> May my meditation be pleasing to him,
> for I rejoice in the LORD.

Some have responded by praising and worshipping nature (Romans 1), but believers of the past call on us to praise Him, the Creator. The heavens do not declare the glory of the heavens. They declare the glory of God. We fall short when our attention ends with what God created. That would be like admiring a painting without taking thought for the talent that produced it. It would be like pointing to something you want to draw someone's attention to, and all they do is stare at your finger.

CONCLUDING REMARKS

Langdon Gilkey writes,

The most fundamental question of religious thought is: who is God—He in whom we put our trust? And the primary answer in both Bible and creed is: 'He is the maker of the heavens and the earth'" (p. 15).

The writer of Hebrews reasons,

For every house is built by someone, but the builder of all things is God" (Hebrews 3:4).

Later, he writes,

"By faith we understand that the universe was created by the word of God, so that which is seen was not made out of things that are visible" (Hebrews 11:3).

God is the Creator of all things: in the heavens and the earth, the sea, and all that is in them. He created all things for His glory.

Our God is in the heavens; He does all that He pleases (Psalm 115:3).

CHAPTER TWO
THE FALL

Act 1: The Creation
Act 2: The Fall
Act 3: The Story of Israel
    God's Promise to Abraham
    The Giving of the Law
    "Give Us a King" (Part 1)
    "Give Us a King" (Part 2)
    The Glory of the Lord Departs
    Return from Captivity
    Second Temple Judaism
Act 4: The Story of Jesus
Act 5: The Story of the Church
Act 6: The Return of the King

The Bible begins with the creation of all things: the universe, all sorts of life, and man. But the story dimension of the Bible does not begin until Genesis 3.

Conflict is, in part, what makes a story a story—no conflict, no story. Some literary scholars affirm that to get to the heart of any story, the reader should identify the conflict(s) as early as possible.

The Conflict of conflicts in the Bible is introduced early. The serpent engages Eve, the mother of all living, in a conversation. He is described as being "more crafty than any other beast of the field that the Lord God had made" (Genesis 3:1). The following lines illustrate his craftiness.

The first words out of his mouth call God into question: "Did God actually say, 'You shall not eat of any tree in the garden'?"

Eve said, "We may eat of the fruit of the trees in the garden, but God said, 'You shall not eat of the fruit of the tree that is in the midst of the garden, neither shall you touch it, lest you die.'"

The serpent contradicts God, "You will not surely die. For God knows that when you eat of it your eyes will be opened, and you will be like God, knowing good and evil."

Satan is the supreme antagonist of the story. He is described as a "serpent." He is "more crafty than any other beast of the field that the Lord God had made" (Genesis 3:1). He is identified in Revelation as "the dragon...that ancient serpent, who is called the devil and Satan" (Revelation 12:9).

Other writers in the Bible comment on the event. For example, Jesus says of Satan, "He was a murderer from the beginning, and has nothing to do with the truth, because there is no truth in him. When he lies, he speaks out of his own character, for he is a liar and the father of lies" (John 8:44).

Paul reflects on the event, "the woman was deceived, and became a transgressor" (1 Timothy 2:14). John reveals the identity of the great dragon as "the ancient serpent, who is called the devil and Satan," and "the deceiver of the whole world" (Revelation

12:9).

Satan's lie held sway over Eve because she lacked faith in what God said, and believed the serpent. In failing to trust God, Eve entertained the notion that God must be withholding some good thing from her. Eve was beguiled into looking at the tree through different eyes. Being tempted, she looked on it as being good for food, a delight to the eyes, and able to make her wise. So, she ate, and gave to her husband, and he ate.

Eve was the one beguiled by the serpent, but it is Adam that God calls on to give answer. Adam blames Eve. Eve blames the serpent. But notice what Paul writes in Romans 5:12,

> Therefore as through one man sin entered into the world and death through sin; for death passed unto all men, for that all sinned.

The Bible singles out Adam.

We may be tempted to go easy on Eve because she was beguiled. But Eve was not blameless. The Lord said to her,

> I will surely multiply your pain in childbearing; in pain you shall bring forth children. Your desire shall be for your husband, and he shall rule over you (Genesis 3:16).

Adam and Eve subjected our world to corruption and decay.

> For the creation waits with eager longing for the revealing of the sons of God. For the creation was subjected to futility, not willingly, but because of him who subjected it, in hope that the creation itself will be set free from its bondage to decay and obtain the freedom of the glory of the children of God. For we know that the whole creation has been groaning

together in the pains of childbirth until now. And not only the creation, but we ourselves, who have the firstfruits of the Spirit, groan inwardly as we wait eagerly for adoption as sons, the redemption of our bodies. For in this hope we were saved. Now hope that is seen is not hope. For who hopes for what he sees? But if we hope for what we do not see, we wait for it with patience (Romans 8:19-25).

COSMIC CONFLICT

A number of conflicts transform this event into a major turning point. There is conflict between:

- Satan and God: in that Satan contradicts the clear teaching of God.

- Satan and Eve: in that Satan does not have Eve's well being at heart. He makes every effort to thwart God's plan for the first human pair.

- Eve and Adam: in that Eve encourages him to partake of the forbidden fruit.

- Eve and God: in that she does not place her confidence in what God said and she allows herself to be beguiled by the devil. God holds her accountable for being beguiled.

- Adam and God: in that, apparently, he knowingly eats of the forbidden fruit.

How does this all tie in to the overall Story of the Bible? In our study of the Creation, I argued that man's supreme purpose in life is to glorify God. When a person violates the will of God they short of glorifying Him (Romans 3:23). Violating the will of God is sin. Adam and Eve fell short of the very purpose for which they were created.

CLASSIC TRAGEDY

The story of the Fall of Adam and Eve provides a paradigm for all tragic stories. Leland Ryken notes, "The plot of tragedy is remarkably constant from one work to another and has six main phases."

> It begins with the hero's *dilemma*, the situation demanding or eliciting a choice. Caught in the difficult position, the tragic hero makes a moral *choice*. The choice plunges both the hero and his world into *catastrophe*. This is accompanied by the tragic hero's *suffering*. Most tragic heroes achieve some type of *perception* near the end of the action. It is an insight into what went wrong (a conviction of sin) and/or an awareness of what the hero has lost by his missing of the mark. The final phase of the tragic plot is normally the *death* of the tragic hero. (145).

Other examples of tragedy in the Bible would include the story of Samson and King Saul.

Let's apply Dr. Ryken's analysis of tragedy to the story of Adam and Eve. Tragedies begin with people in high or exalted positions. Adam and Eve are in the Garden of Eden, walking with God in the cool of the garden, enjoying intimate fellowship with their Creator.

The *dilemma* comes when the serpent tempts Eve into thinking differently about her divine provisions. Should she restrict herself from eating of the tree of the knowledge of good and evil, or should she partake, and "be like God knowing good and evil"?

Eve *chooses* to eat—and she gives to her husband, and he eats.

Now comes the *catastrophe*. They are banished from the Garden of Eden, thus restricting their access to the tree of life. No longer having access to the tree of life, they, of course, are cursed to die.

And not only does their choice bring catastrophe upon them, but by them, the entire world is subjected to corruption and death (Romans 5:12).

So far as gaining any *perception* or insight about what they did, God confronts them and pronounces specific judgments against each party involved: Adam, Eve, and the Serpent. Part of the Lord's judgment against them involved banishment from the Garden lest they eat of the tree of life and live forever. Death entered the world through sin (Romans 5:12).

IMPORTANCE

God created the universe in His good pleasure and for His glory. He created man to live forever. But when Adam and Eve violated God's will by partaking of the forbidden tree, death entered the picture. Paul writes, "Therefore, as through one man sin entered into the world and death through sin, so that death passed unto all men, for that all sin" (Romans 5:12). We die because of what happened in the beginning, in the Garden of Eden. In another place, Paul describes death as "the last enemy to be destroyed" (1 Corinthians 15:26).

Consider the explanatory power of the Genesis account. It explains why we die. Peter Kreeft introduced his book on the subject of death by writing,

> The questions What is death? and Why do we die? are the deepest of all questions. They are questions the poet, the philosopher, the mystic, and the child ask; and they are questions the poet, philosopher, mystic, and child in each of us asks. We keep asking. (Kreeft, p. xv).

The book of Genesis provides us with an answer. Death is

separation from God as evidenced in the mortality of man. The reason we die is because of what happened in the garden, coupled with our own propensity to sin "for all sin" (Romans 5:12).

"EUCATASTROPHE"

Tragedies end in death. A classic Comedy, on the other hand, does not end in death. Comedies follow the same pattern as Tragedies with a hero who must make a choice. They make the wrong choice, plunging their world into catastrophe. There is a moment of awareness, an epiphany, but, ultimately, the hero dies. In a comedy, the hero does not die.

Every one of our lives is or was a tragedy in the making. We, like the tragic hero, desired the wrong thing. The Bible calls it sin. When the gospel is preached, the nature of our choice is made clear to us. If we respond properly to God's love, the tragedy is averted, and our tragic story is converted into a comedy. (This is no laughing matter.) J.R.R. Tolkien coined the word "eucatastrophe" to name it.

CHAPTER THREE

THE PROMISE

Act 1: The Creation
Act 2: The Fall
Act 3: The Story of Israel
    God's Promise to Abraham
    The Giving of the Law
    "Give Us a King" (Part 1)
    "Give Us a King" (Part 2)
    The Glory of the Lord Departs
    Return from Captivity
    Second Temple Judaism
Act 4: The Story of Jesus
Act 5: The Story of the Church
Act 6: The Return of the King

God created the heavens and the earth, the sea and all that in them is (Exodus 20:11). "He spoke, and it came to be; he commanded and it stood firm" (Psalm 33:9). "By faith we understand that the universe was created by the word of God, so that what is seen was not made out of things that are visible" (Hebrews 11:3).

God created everything for His good pleasure; for the purpose of glorifying Him. The heavens are doing a splendid job fulfilling their mission (Psalm 19:1), but man has fallen short. Paul affirms that all have sinned and fall short of the glory of God (Romans 3:23), and the just wages for having missed the mark is death (Romans 6:23).

The Story of the Bible is God's full presentation of the Gospel. More specifically, the word "gospel" means "good news," and the good news is all about Jesus (1 Corinthians 15:3ff; 2 Tim 2:8) The fact that all have sinned, and fall short of the glory of God, and deserve to die is horribly bad news. So, where does the good news come in? I am sad to say it gets worse before it gets better.

THREE CATACLYSMIC SCENES

The first eleven chapters of Genesis record three cataclysmic judgment scenes. The first one was discussed in our last lesson under the heading of the Fall (Genesis 3; Romans 5:12).

The second is recorded in Genesis 6-9, and centers on the flood of Noah's day. Moses writes,

> The Lord saw that the wickedness of man was great in the earth, and that every intention of the thoughts of his heart was only evil continually. And the Lord was sorry that he had made man on the earth, and it grieved him to his heart (Gen 6:5, 6).

So, God called Noah to build an ark whereby eight souls were saved through water (1 Peter 3:21). Through the flood God determined to make an end of all flesh (Genesis 6:11f).

The flood,

> ...blotted out every living thing that was on the face of the ground, men and animals and creeping things and birds of the heavens. They were blotted out from the earth. Only Noah was left, and those who were with him in the ark (7:23).

The third of these events is recorded in Genesis chapter eleven where God's judgment is executed against man for seeking to make a name for himself at the tower of Babel. God's command in the beginning was to "be fruitful and multiply and fill the earth" (Genesis 1:28). One of the motives for building the tower is expressed in Genesis 11:4,

> Come, let us build ourselves a city and a tower with its top in the heavens, and let us make a name for ourselves, lest we be dispersed over the face of the whole earth.

So, God confounded their language and scattered mankind over the face of all the earth (11:8).

These three history-altering world-wide cataclysmic events lead the reader to the promise God gives to Abraham. N. T. Wright observes...

> ...the entire Old Testament as we have it hangs like an enormous door on a small hinge, namely the call of Abraham in Genesis 12. This, it appears, is intended by God the Creator to address the problem evident in Genesis 3 (human rebellion and the expulsion from the Garden of Eden), Genesis 6-7 (human wickedness and the flood) and Genesis 11 (human arrogance, the tower of Babel and the confusion of languages). (46, 2006).

From creation to *human rebellion*, *human wickedness,* and *human arrogance* the Prologue highlights humanities' problem. What is the solution? This is the question the Story answers.

THE PROMISE

God's call of Abraham is a major turning point in the Story of the Bible. If the reader does not see the import of the promise given to Abraham as it relates the whole story, it tends to reduce the individual episodes of the Bible into a number of disconnected unrelated events. Stories are typically reduced into a host of moral tales.

Please pay careful attention to this text,

> Now the LORD said to Abram, "Go from your country and your kindred and your father's house to the land that I will show you. And I will make of you a great nation, and I will bless you and make your name great, so that you will be a blessing. I will bless those who bless you, and him who dishonors you I will curse, and in you all the families of the earth shall be blessed."

> So Abram went, as the LORD had told him, and Lot went with him. Abram was seventy-five years old when he departed from Haran. And Abram took Sarai his wife, and Lot his brother's son, and all their possessions that they had gathered, and the people that they had acquired in Haran, and they set out to go to the land of Canaan. When they came to the land of Canaan, Abram passed through the land to the place at Shechem, to the oak of Moreh. At that time the Canaanites were in the land. Then the LORD appeared to Abram and said, "To your offspring I will give this land." So he built there an altar to the LORD, who had appeared to him. From there he moved to the hill country on the east of Bethel and pitched his tent, with Bethel on the west and Ai on the east. And there he built an altar to the LORD

30

and called upon the name of the LORD. And Abram journeyed on, still going toward the Negeb (Genesis 12:1-9).

God's promise to Abraham is multifaceted. God said,

- I will make of you a great nation.
- I will bless you and make your name great, so that you will be a blessing.
- I will bless them who bless you, and him who dishonors you I will curse.
- In you all the families of the earth shall be blessed.
- To your offspring I will give this land

The condition that activates these blessings is clear, "Go from your country and your kindred and your father's house to the land that I will show you."

"So Abram went." The significance of these three words escaped me until I read Thomas Cahill's comments in his book, *The Gift of the Jews*. He argues that the words "Abram went" are "two of the boldest words in all literature."

They signal a complete departure from everything that has gone before in the long evolution of culture and sensibility. Out of Sumer, civilized repository of the predictable, comes a man who does not know where he is going but goes forth into the unknown wilderness under the prompting of his God. Out of Mesopotamia, home of canny, self-serving merchants who use their gods to ensure prosperity and favor, comes a wealthy caravan with no material goal. Out of ancient humanity, which from the dim beginnings of its consciousness has read its eternal verities in the stars, comes a party traveling by no known compass. Out of the human race, which knows in its bones that all its striving must end in death, comes a leader who says he has been given an impossible promise. Out of mortal imagination comes a dream of something new, something better, something yet to happen, something—in the future (63, 1998).

"He does not know where he is going," but he knows Who is leading. "He left with no material goal," but "He was looking forward to the city that has foundations, whose designer and builder is God" (Hebrews 11:10). He left "traveling by no known compass," but God said, "I will show you." He is given "an impossible promise," but,

> He did not weaken in faith when he considered his own body, which was as good as dead (since he was about a hundred years old), or when he considered the barrenness of Sarah's womb. No distrust made him waver concerning the promise of God, but he grew strong in his faith as he gave glory to God, feeling convinced that God was able to do what he had promised (Romans 4:19-21).

God promised to draw a nation out of the loins of a one hundred year old man. He actually produced two nations from Abraham, one through Ishmael, the other through Isaac. Isaac was the son according to promise.

The promise to make of Abraham a great nation, and to give him land was primarily for the purpose of preserving Abraham's family till the seed should come. Abraham begat Isaac, and Isaac begat Jacob. Jacob's name was changed to Israel, and Israel had twelve sons. These twelve sons flourished into tribes and so we have the twelve tribes of Israel. In particular, it was through the tribe of Judah that the Christ would come.

Moses' account of world history is not cyclical like the stories the pagan nations told. He does not paint a picture of things simply repeating themselves in an endless cycle. Mr. Cahill titled his book *The Gift of the Jews*. That gift, he argues, is a story that breaks out of the endless cycle portrayed by the pagans. N. T. Wright concurs, "...the Christian story isn't about time going round and round in circles, but about time going forward into God's new world" (69, 2003).

THE SIGNIFICANCE OF THE PROMISE

The preservation of the seed of Abraham is important because it is through Abraham that the Messiah would come, and thus fulfill God's promise to Abraham. God said to Abram, "and in you all the families of the earth shall be blessed" (22:16).

Paul comments on this promise:

> And the scripture, foreseeing that God would justify the Gentiles by faith, preached the gospel beforehand to Abraham, saying, in you shall the nations of the earth be blessed. So then, those who are of faith are blessed along with Abraham, the man of faith (Gal 3:8, 9).

When God promised to bless all the families of the earth through Abraham's seed, he was preaching the gospel—the good news. When the promise is repeated to Abraham in Genesis 22:18, the Lord said, "In your offspring shall all the nations of the earth be blessed." Paul draws us in for a closer look: "It does not say, 'and to offsprings,' referring to many, but referring to one, 'And to your offspring,' who is Christ" (Gal 3:16).

When you add it all up, Paul is saying that in Christ shall all the nations of the earth be blessed."

What is the promised blessing? Peter spells it out for us in his second recorded sermon in the book of Acts,

> Unto you first God, having raised up his Servant, sent him to bless you, in turning away every one of you from your iniquities" (Acts 3:25, 26).

CHAPTER FOUR
THE GIVING OF THE LAW

Before we enter into the account of the Exodus and the giving of the Law, some historical background is in order. The last "turning point" centered on Abraham leaving the city of Ur to go to a land God promised to give him and his descendants. The promise God made to Abraham (Genesis 12) is repeated to his son, Isaac (Genesis 26), and to Isaac's son,

Jacob (Genesis 28). Jacob had twelve sons. They grew in number to eventually make up the nation of Israel.

One of the subplots among the stories about these twelve tribes centers on one of the twelve sons. The story of Joseph (Genesis 37-50) links the book of Genesis to the book of Exodus. Joseph is sold into slavery by his jealous brothers. Joseph goes from rags to riches rising to a position second to Pharaoh. While Joseph is in Egypt, a famine arises back home in Canaan. Some of his brothers travel to Egypt in search of food. They do not recognize Joseph at first due to the time that separated them from the last meeting. Joseph tests his brothers and, eventually, embraces them. He interprets all of the circumstances surrounding him, including their betrayal of him, as something God used to preserve Abraham's seed. Joseph beckons his family to Egypt. He dies and a Pharaoh who knew not Joseph arises. The descendants of Abraham find themselves enslaved, and conditions go from bad to worse. They call on God for deliverance, and God uses Moses to lead them out of Egypt.

THE GIVING OF THE LAW

> On the third new moon after the people of Israel had gone out of the land of Egypt, on that day they came into the wilderness of Sinai. They set out from Rephidim and came into the wilderness of Sinai, and they encamped in the wilderness. There Israel encamped before the mountain, while Moses went up to God. (Exodus 19:1, 2).

Moses is careful to describe the time setting in order to show that the covenant given at Sinai was given on the fiftieth day of Israel's Exodus from Egypt. Israel arrived in the wilderness of Sinai on the forty-eighth day after they left Egypt. The forty-ninth day they set up camp at the mountain. The next day, the fiftieth, Moses receives the Law. When you tie in these time calculations with the time reference given in Numbers 10:11, Israel would have been at the foot of Mt. Sinai for nearly one year.

Another point of interest: when God spoke to Moses at the burning bush, he said, "when you have brought the people out of Egypt, you shall serve God on this mountain" (3:12).

MOUNT SINAI

The scene described in Exodus 19 and 20 is momentous and unforgettable. Moses makes three treks to the top of the mountain. On the first trip, the Lord tells Moses to say to the people,

> You yourselves have seen what I did to the Egyptians, and how I bore you on eagles' wings and brought you to myself. Now therefore, if you will indeed obey my voice and keep my covenant, you shall be my treasured possession among all peoples, for all the earth is mine; and you shall be to me a kingdom of priests and a holy nation. These are the words that you shall speak to the people of Israel." So Moses came and called the elders of the people and set before them all these words that the LORD had commanded him (Exodus 19:4-7).

When Moses delivers this message to the people, they say, "All that the LORD has spoken we will do." When Moses reports back to God, He says, "Behold, I am coming to you in a thick cloud, that the people may hear when I speak with you, and may also believe you forever" (19:9).

On the second trip to the top of the mountain, Moses is sent back to tell the people to prepare themselves for the reception of God's law (19:11-15). They are to wash their garments and set bounds for the people to keep them from touching the border of it:

> Take care not to go up into the mountain or touch the edge of it. Whoever touches the mountain shall be put to death. No hand shall touch him, but it shall be stoned or shot; whether beast or man, he shall not live (19:12, 13).

All of this was in preparation for the third day (19:11-15).

> On the morning of the third day there were thunders and lightenings and a thick cloud on the mountain and a very loud trumpet blast, so that all the people in the camp trembled. Then Moses brought the people out of the camp to meet God, and they took their stand at the foot of the mountain. Now Mount Sinai was wrapped in smoke because the LORD had descended on it in fire. The smoke of it went up like the smoke of a kiln, and the whole mountain trembled greatly. And as the sound of the trumpet grew louder and louder, Moses spoke, and God answered him in thunder. The LORD came down on Mount Sinai, to the top of the mountain. And the LORD called Moses to the top of the mountain, and Moses went up (19:16-20).

God charges Moses to return to the people to command them, again, not to break through the set boundaries in order to gaze upon God. So, Moses descends to remind the people not to cross the boundaries set for them. It is at this point in the narrative that God speaks the Ten Commandments (20:3-17).

THE PEOPLE'S REACTION

There were thunderings and lightenings, and the voice of the trumpet, and the mountain smoked. Apparently, the sound of this mysterious trumpet grew louder and louder (19:19). The people trembled and stood afar off, saying to Moses, "Speak to us yourself and we will listen; but let not God speak to us, or we will die" (20:19).

These sights and sounds filled men's hearts with dread. It is what unholy men feel when they perceive that they are in the presence of the holy God of heaven. It is what Isaiah felt when he was in the temple (Isaiah 6). It is what Peter felt when he became aware of the fact that he stood in the presence of the Lord (Luke 5:1-11).

Moses tried to calm them, "Do not fear; for God has come to test you, and that His fear may be before you, so that you may not sin" (Exodus 20:20).

The fear that struck the children of Israel was natural for anyone standing in the presence of God, but it was also due to the wickedness that resided in their hearts. Prior to the giving of the Law, the people said, "All that the Lord hath spoken we will do" (10:8), but on one of Moses' subsequent trips to the top of Sinai, Israel was in the process of violating several of God's commands. God's awesome presence was designed to set His fear before them so that they sin not (20:20). It was to prove them. They failed the test shortly thereafter. Failure, generally, characterizes their long history.

THE SIGNIFICANCE OF THE EXODUS

Moses looks back at the events surrounding Israel's Exodus

from Egypt in Deuteronomy 4. He argues that the Lord's calling of Israel is based on the Lord's unique work in the Exodus, the giving of the Law, and how Israel's life is to reflect their Lord's unique work.

> For ask now of the days that are past, which were before you, since the day that God created man on the earth, and ask from one end of heaven to the other, whether such a great thing as this has ever happened or was ever heard of. Did any people ever hear the voice of a god speaking out of the midst of the fire, as you have heard, and still live? Or has any god ever attempted to go and take a nation for himself from the midst of another nation, by trials, by signs, by wonders, and by war, by a mighty hand and an outstretched arm, and by great deeds of terror, all of which the LORD your God did for you in Egypt before your eyes? To you it was shown, that you might know that the LORD is God; there is no other besides him. Out of heaven he let you hear his voice, that he might discipline you. And on earth he let you see his great fire, and you heard his words out of the midst of the fire. And because he loved your fathers and chose their offspring after them and brought you out of Egypt with his own presence, by his great power, driving out before you nations greater and mightier than yourselves, to bring you in, to give you their land for an inheritance, as it is this day, know therefore today, and lay it to your heart, that the LORD is God in heaven above and on the earth beneath; there is no other. Therefore you shall keep his statutes and his commandments, which I command you today, that it may go well with you and with your children after you, and that you may prolong your days in the land that the LORD your God is giving you for all time (4:32-40).

This speech is rooted in historical experience and in the ethical demands it places on Israel. It encompasses the whole of human history, "since the day that God created man on the earth." And it encompasses the whole of mankind, "ask from one end of heaven to the other…"

The "great thing" Moses speaks of encompasses the Exodus and the giving of the Law. His claim is that nothing like this has ever happened. It was unprecedented. It is not just that the Lord has done this great thing, but that no god had ever done anything like it.

The purpose of this "great thing" is explained in 4:35, "To you it was shown, that you might know that the LORD [YHWH] is God; there is no other besides him" (4:35). The question of God's existence is not as important here as is His identity. That there is no god but one is a prominent theme stated over and over again in the Bible—not just in the Old Testament (Deuteronomy 6:4), but also in the New Testament (Ephesians 4:4-6).

The Exodus of the children of Israel out of Egypt and the giving of the Law, together, function as a turning point in the Story the Bible tells. Every Sabbath looked back to it. As you read the Bible for yourself, notice how often this event is referenced.

As a case in point, consider the remarks of Rahab of Jericho. Remember, she was a pagan woman and a harlot. She lived in the land Israel entered to possess. She says to the two spies:

> I know that the LORD has given you the land, and that the fear of you has fallen upon us, and that all the inhabitants of the land melt away before you. For we have heard how the Lord dried up the water of the Red Sea before you when you came out of Egypt, and what you did to the two kings of the Amorites who were beyond the Jordan, to Sihon

and Og, whom you devoted to destruction. And as soon as we heard it, our hearts melted, and there was no spirit left in any man because of you, for the LORD your God, he is God in the heavens above and on the earth beneath. Now then, please swear to me by the LORD that, as I have dealt kindly with you, you also will deal kindly with my father's house, and give me a sure sign that you will save alive my father and mother, my brothers and sisters, and all who belong to them, and deliver our lives from death." And the men said to her, "Our life for yours even to death! If you do not tell this business of ours, then when the LORD gives us the land we will deal kindly and faithfully with you (Joshua 2:9-14).

Some have argued that the language used in the New Testament, describing the Christian's deliverance from sin, hearkens back to the Exodus of Israel out of Egypt. Paul uses expressions like, "…enslaved to sin…set free from sin…" and sin no longer exercising dominion over us—all in Romans 6. Judge for yourself.

CONCLUDING REMARKS

Some novelists write stories imagining how different our world would be if some significant event in history had turned out differently. Philip K. Dick wrote an alternative history imagining what the United States might be like if the Japanese had won World War II. I would like for you to imagine how different Israel's history could have been if God had not given them the Law.

The giving of the Law at Mt. Sinai carries with it huge ramifications, not only for the nation of Israel, but for the world. By Israel's faithful obedience to the Law, they would function as light to the nations. The tribe of Levi functioned as priests among the twelve tribes of Israel. The nation of Israel was to function as priests among the various nations of the earth.

Much of what Paul writes in Romans 2 is an indictment against Israel failing their priestly function to be a light to the world. The Lord judged the Jews for their failure and condemned them along with the Gentiles. In chapter 3 Paul anticipates the question: "What advantage has the Jew?" (3:1). He responds, "Much in every way. To begin with, the Jews were entrusted with the oracles of God" (3:2).

CHAPTER FIVE
"GIVE US A KING" (1)

Man never seems to be content with what he has. Solomon describes the problem in Ecclesiastes:

All things are full of weariness:
a man cannot utter it;

the eye is not satisfied with seeing
nor the ear filled with hearing (1:8)

The same could be said of money. The word "enough" is rarely used in the same breath as the word "money."

Couple this idea from Ecclesiastes with the desire to be like everyone else. This impulse can be seen in school children and their desire to look like everyone else in school. A trend is set, and our children quickly feel the pressure to be like everyone else—to wear what they wear, to like what they like, to dislike what others dislike. This is not a problem restricted to children.

Israel of old was no different. A major turning point in her history occurs when she expresses the desire to be "like all the nations" (1 Sam. 8:5).

GIVE US A KING

God led the children of Israel out of Egypt and into the wilderness by Moses. Shortly after their Exodus from Egypt, the Lord delivered His Law. Israel remained in the wilderness for 40 years. This was the punishment decreed by God for the unbelief they exhibited after being delivered from over 400 years of slavery in Egypt. Moses dies, and Joshua leads them into the Promised Land.

The period of time following Israel's entrance into the Promised Land is recorded in the book of Judges. This had to be Israel's "nadir," meaning the low point in her history. The book of Judges records a series of cycles in Israel's story. Israel makes a mess of things, God stirs up one of the foreign nations to chastise her. Israel cries out for deliverance. God raises up a

Judge, or Savior, to deliver them, and they enjoy a time of peace for a season—only to make a mess of things again, for God to stir up another foreign nation, for Israel to cry out, for God to raise up another Judge to deliver them, and for them to enjoy a time of peace again. This pattern is repeated numerous times in the book.

Samuel is the last Judge in Israel. When he was old his sons did not walk in his ways (1 Samuel 8:5). "They took bribes and perverted justice" (8:3). So, the people said, "Now appoint for us a king to judge us like the nations" (8:5).

> But the thing displeased Samuel when they said, "Give us a king to judge us." So Samuel prayed to the LORD. And the LORD said to Samuel, "Heed the voice of the people in all that they say to you; for they have not rejected you, but they have rejected Me, that I should not reign over them. According to all the works which they have done since the day that I brought them up out of Egypt, even to this day— with which they have forsaken Me and served other gods—so they are doing to you also. Now therefore, heed their voice. However, you shall solemnly forewarn them, and show them the behavior of the king who will reign over them" (8:6-9).

They rejected God from being king over them.

Samuel tells them how their lives will be different under a human ruler (1 Samuel 8:10-18):

> This will be the behavior of the king who will reign over you: He will take your sons and appoint *them* for his own chariots and *to be* his horsemen, and *some* will run before his chariots. He will appoint captains over his thousands and captains over his fifties, *will set some* to plow his ground and reap his harvest, and *some* to make his weapons of

war and equipment for his chariots. He will take your daughters *to be* perfumers, cooks, and bakers. And he will take the best of your fields, your vineyards, and your olive groves, and give *them* to his servants. He will take a tenth of your grain and your vineyards, and give it to his officers and servants. And he will take your male servants, your female servants, your finest young men, and your donkeys, and put *them* to his work. He will take a tenth of your sheep. And you will be his servants. And you will cry out in that day because of your king whom you have chosen for yourselves, and the LORD will not hear you in that day."

But the people refuse to obey, and say, "No, but we will have a king over us that we also may be like the nations, and that our king may judge us and go out before us and fight our battles" (1 Samuel 8:19, 20).

I see three identifiable phases to the issue of kingship in Israel as it plays itself out in the Story of the Bible. First, there is God's law concerning kings—given on the eve of their entrance into the Promised Land. Second, there is the selection of a king, and the succession of kings in Israel's history. Finally, there is the One whom God appoints to sit on David's throne forever, a promise made to David and fulfilled in Jesus at His ascension and exaltation at the right hand of the throne of God.

GOD'S LAW CONCERNING KINGS

Deuteronomy literally means, "the law again." It is a summary or recap of the Story "thus far." It retells the story of the giving of the law, so the Greek title of the book is "the law again," or *deutero* (again) *nomos* (law). It warns Israel of the dangers that await them in the Promised Land, and exhorts them to remain faithful to God by keeping His commandments.

In chapter 17, there are two paragraphs that concern Israel's future kings:

> When you come to the land that the LORD your God is giving you, and you possess it, and dwell in it and then say, ' I will set a king over me, like all the nations that are around me,' you may indeed set a king over you whom the LORD your God will choose. One from among your brothers you shall set as king over you. You may not put a foreigner over you, who is not your brother. Only he must not acquire many horses for himself or cause the people to return to Egypt in order to acquire many horses, since the LORD has said to you, 'You shall never return that way again.' And he shall not acquire many wives for himself, lest his heart turn away, nor shall he acquire for himself excessive silver and gold.

> And when he sits on the throne of his kingdom, he shall write for himself in a book a copy of this law, approved by the Levitical priests. And it shall be with him, and he shall read in it all the days of his life, that he may learn to fear the LORD his God by keeping all the words of this law and these statutes, and doing them, that his heart may not be lifted up above his brothers, and that he may not turn aside from the commandment, either to the right hand or to the left, so that he may continue long in his kingdom, he and his children, in Israel (Deuteronomy 17:14-20).

The Lord predicts their desire and request for a king. He gives them permission to set a king over them, but the king is to be one of God's choosing.

It might make for an interesting study to compare the various kings of Israel with the standard set in Deuteronomy 17 to see how many of them lived up to it. I will save you the trouble. None of them did. In fact, you can see where each of them went astray by comparing them with the mandates of the above two paragraphs.

For example, consider Solomon, a man described as the wisest who ever lived. He loved many foreign women, along with the daughter of Pharaoh. It was his wives that turned his heart away from God (1 Kings. 11:2). He multiplied to himself wives and princesses and concubines—1,000 total. "So Solomon did what was evil in the sight of the LORD and he did not wholly follow the LORD, as David his father had done" (1 Kings 11:6).

When the people asked for a king they rejected God as King. God was their presiding King. As far back in Israel's history as the Exodus from Egypt, God functioned as King. The song sung by the nation after passing through the Red Sea exalts God by saying there is no one like him:

> Who is like you, O LORD, among the gods? Who is like you, majestic in holiness, awesome in glorious deeds, doing wonders?" (Exodus 15:11).

The song catalogues the many times the LORD delivered Israel from her enemies, and ends with these words, "The LORD will reign forever and ever" (v 18). Miriam sang,

> Sing to the LORD, for he has triumphed gloriously; the horse and his rider he has thrown into the sea (v 21).

Zechariah foretells of a time when

everyone who survives of all the nations that have come against Jerusalem shall go up year after year to worship the King, the LORD of hosts, and to keep the Feast of Booths (Zechariah 14:16).

Through the pen of Malachi, the Lord says,

I am a great King, says the LORD of hosts, and my name will be feared among the nations (1:14).

First Samuel 8 records Israel's demand for a king. Their request implies their rejection of God as King. Saul is Israel's first human-king. He is, eventually, rejected by God as Israel's king, because he did not obey the Lord in utterly destroying the Amalekites, Samuel says,

Has the LORD *as great* delight in burnt offerings and sacrifices,
As in obeying the voice of the LORD?
Behold, to obey is better than sacrifice,
And to heed than the fat of rams.
For rebellion *is as* the sin of witchcraft,
And stubbornness *is as* iniquity and idolatry.
Because you have rejected the word of the LORD,
He also has rejected you from *being* king (1 Samuel 15:22-23).

All the kings of Israel were given by way of concession. Their corruption stands in stark contrast with the king of God's ultimate choosing.

In the next chapter, we will see how this issue of Israel's desire for a king ultimately plays itself out in God becoming King of Israel again—King not of Israel only, but of all mankind.

CHAPTER SIX
"GIVE US A KING" (2)

In April 2002, the church in Chino sent me to Northern Ireland with Don Ruhl to work with a small church in Belfast. The reason I say "Northern Ireland" is not to distinguish it from other geographical regions of Ireland, though the description is accurate. It is a political distinction. "Northern Ireland" is called so because it is under British rule unlike the rest of Ireland.

Margaret was a woman in her eighties. She delighted living under British rule. Not everyone shared her enthusiasm. As you can imagine, there were others in Northern Ireland that opposed British rule.

When Don and I first visited with Margaret, she shared her political views and eloquently defended them. We listened with equal politeness, but whether Northern Ireland was under British or Irish rule had little to do with the reason for our visit. And whether that region of the island was under British or Irish rule had no impact on our mission. We were there to tell her about Jesus, who is King of kings and Lord of lords, and to encourage her to be baptized into His kingdom and to embrace His ethics for living.

This is how I feel about living in the United States, though the parallel is not identical. We live in a nation with two prominent political parties. Election for President occurs every 4 years. One man wins and others lose, but the work of the church does not change. We still serve Jesus of Nazareth, our King and Lord, the One whose kingdom shall not be shaken or left to another. That will never change. We live according to the laws of our land, and pray for her leaders "…that we may lead a peaceful and quiet life, godly and dignified in every way" (1 Tim. 2:3). We are to be the salt of the earth and the light of the world, broadcasting the word.

In the last chapter, I identified one of the dozen or so primary turning points in the Story of the Bible. It is recorded in 1 Samuel 8. Israel cries out for a king in order to be like the nations around her (1 Samuel 8:5). The elders of Israel went to Ramah, and said to Samuel,

> Behold, you are old and your sons do not walk in your ways. Now appoint for us a king to judge us like all the nations.

Samuel was very displeased. He prayed to the Lord. The Lord said, "obey the voice of the people..." And He said, "they have not rejected you, but they have rejected me from being king over them" (8:7). If memory serves me correctly, I have always remembered the part of this verse that reads, "they have rejected me," but I did not recall the clause, "from being king over them." This is too significant a clause for me to have forgotten.

When we consider the kings of Israel we do not find a single ideal king. The best of them was David—but even he had his flaws.

Here is the important point I want you to consider. All the kings of Israel were given by way of concession. The corrupt kings of Israel are a stark contrast with the King of God's ultimate choosing. Jesus' rule and reign as Lord of lords, and King of kings, being seated at God's right hand with all authority in heaven and on earth, is intended to reestablish the rule of God as sovereign King.

Let's develop this idea further. First of all, let's take a look at Jesus' reign as foretold by the prophets. Then, let's take a look at the emphasis in the New Testament on Jesus as King. And finally, let's firm up the reality of Jesus' reign as King today.

JESUS' REIGN IN PROPHECY

On his deathbed, Abraham's grandson, Jacob, called his sons to his side to tell them what would befall them in the latter days (Genesis 49:1). He prophesies concerning the future of each of his sons. Of Judah, he says,

> Judah is a lion's cub; from the prey, my son, you have gone up. He stooped down; he crouched as a lion and as a lioness; who dares rouse him? The scepter shall not depart from Judah, nor the ruler's staff from between his feet, until tribute comes to him; and to him shall be the obedience of the peoples (Genesis 49:9, 10).

Not much could be known concerning the significance of this prophetic utterance at the time it was spoken. But it does make sense when you trace Judah's history.

One of the key players in Judah's history is David, King of Israel. A pivotal event in David's life is recorded in 2 Samuel 7. David is the reigning king at the time and God has given him rest from all of his enemies. David expresses his awkwardness at dwelling in a house of cedar while the ark of God dwelt within curtains. He wants to build a house for the Lord. Nathan, the prophet, tells David, "Go, do all that is in your heart, for the Lord is with you" (2 Samuel 7:3).

Nathan receives an additional word from God for David concerning the king's desire to build a house for the Lord. God promises to build a house for David.

> And I will give you rest from all your enemies. Moreover, the Lord declares to you that the Lord will make you a house. When your days are fulfilled and you lie down with your fathers, I will raise up your

offspring after you, who shall come from your body, and I will establish his kingdom. He shall build a house for my name, and I will establish the throne of his kingdom forever. I will be to him a father, and he shall be to me a son. When he commits iniquity, I will discipline him with the rod of men, with the stripes of the sons of men, but my steadfast love will not depart from him, as I took it from Saul, whom I put away from before you. And your house and your kingdom shall be made sure forever before me. Your throne shall be established forever. In accordance with all this vision Nathan spoke to David (2 Sam. 7:11-17) .

David went in, sat before the Lord, and poured out his heartfelt gratitude for these divine blessings (2 Samuel 7:18-29).

First, God promises to establish David's throne forever. Solomon reigned after his father, David, and other kings followed. The Lord said, "Your throne shall be established forever" (7:16). This promise is ultimately fulfilled in Jesus, the Christ, in whom the kingdom was forever established.

Second, notice that the promise was to be fulfilled after David's death and while David was in the tomb. Nathan says, "When your days are fulfilled and you lie down with your fathers, I will raise up your offspring after you, who shall come from your body, and I will establish his kingdom" (7:12). Peter, on the day of Pentecost, highlights this very thing:

Brothers, I may say to you with confidence about the patriarch David that he both died and was buried, and his tomb is with us to this day. Being therefore a prophet, and knowing that God had sworn with an oath to him that he would set one of his descendants on his throne, he foresaw and spoke about the resurrection of the Christ, that he was not abandoned to Hades, nor did his flesh see corruption. This Jesus

God raised up, and of that we all are witnesses. Being therefore exalted at the right hand of God, and having received from the Father the promise of the Holy Spirit he has poured out this that you yourselves are seeing and hearing. For David did not ascend into the heavens, but he himself says,

'The Lord said to my lord,
Sit at my right hand,
    until I make your enemies your footstool.' (Acts 2:29-36).

Jacob foretold that the scepter would not depart out of Judah. David was of the tribe of Judah, and king over Israel. Scepters and kingdoms go hand in hand. Jesus was a descendant of David, thus of the tribe of Judah. He is the ultimate fulfillment of the promise of God to David.

There are two other texts that should be read in light of what has just been said. The first text is Psalm 89:19-37. In this passage, the poet rehearses God's promise to establish David's throne forever.

Once for all I have sworn by my holiness;
    I will not lie to David.
His offspring shall endure forever,
    his throne as long as the sun before me.
Like the moon it shall be established forever,
    a faithful witness in the skies (Psalm 89:35-37).

The second text is Acts 2:22-36. This text is Peter's sermon on the first Pentecost after the resurrection of Jesus. Every point in the sermon centers on Jesus:

1.   Jesus was a man approved of by God (2:22)

2. He was delivered up (2:23)

3. He was crucified and slain (2:23)

4. God raised Him from the dead (2:24)

5. He ascended on high where He was and remains exalted at the right hand of God (2:32-35)

Peter concludes,

Let all the house of Israel therefore know for certain that God has made him both Lord and Christ, this Jesus whom you crucified" (Acts 2:36).

When you read these two texts in light of the promise God made to Judah and to David the following can be tied together:

1. Jacob prophesied that the scepter would not depart from Judah.

2. David was of the tribe of Judah.

3. God swore with an oath that he would establish David's kingdom forever—"that the fruit of his loins he would set upon his throne"

4. Peter argues that this is a reference to the resurrection, ascension and enthronement of Christ at God's right hand.

Conclusion: Jesus is seated on David's throne forever.

JESUS: KING OF THE JEWS

John's account of the gospel begins by tells us about the recruiting of Jesus' disciples, Nathanael being one of them. Nathanael is the one who said, "Can anything good come out of

Nazareth?" (John 1:46). When Nathanael came to Jesus, the Lord said, "Behold, an Israelite indeed, in whom there is no deceit!"

Nathanael said, "How do you know me?"

Jesus said, "Before Philip called you, when you were under the fig tree, I saw you."

Nathanael confesses, "Rabbi, you are the Son of God! You are the King of Israel!" (1:49). What did Nathanael have in mind when he referred to Jesus as "King of Israel"?

After the feeding of the 5,000, Jesus perceived that they were about to take Him by force to make him king, so He withdrew again to the mountain by Himself to avoid the incident (6:15).

When Jesus entered Jerusalem toward the end of the gospel accounts, the people took branches of palm trees and met him, crying out, "Hosanna! Blessed is he who comes in the name of the Lord, even the King of Israel!" John relates this to a prophecy in Zechariah 9:9,

> Fear not, daughter of Zion; behold, your king is coming, sitting on a donkey's colt!

When on trial, Pilate asks Jesus, "Are you the King of the Jews?" (18:33). After a brief exchange, Jesus says,

> "My kingdom is not of this world, If my kingdom were of this world, my servants would have been fighting, that I might not be delivered over to the Jews. But my kingdom is not from the world" (18:36).

When Pilate asks, "So you are King?" Jesus answers,

You say that I am a king. For this purpose I was born and for this purpose I have come into the world—to bear witness to the truth. Everyone who is of the truth listens to my voice (18:37).

Luke 1:26-33 records the angel's announcement to Mary concerning a son. When Mary sings her song of praise (Luke 1:46-55), one line reads,

> He has shown strength with his arm;
> he has scattered the proud in the thoughts of their hearts;
> he has brought down the mighty from their thrones and exalted those
> of humble estate... (1:51).

When an angel of the Lord announces the birth of Jesus to the shepherds in the field, he says,

> Fear not, for behold, I bring you good news of great joy that will be for all the people. For unto you is born this day in the city of David, a Savior, who is Christ the Lord" (Luke 2:10, 11).

Back to John's account of the Gospel. The Roman soldiers twisted together a crown of thorns, put it on His head, and arrayed Him in a purple robe. They mocked him, saying, "Hail, King of the Jews," and then beat Him (19:3).

While on trial, the Jews tried to worsen Jesus' case before Pilate, a Roman official, by saying, "If you release this man, you are not Caesar's friend. Everyone who makes himself a king opposes Caesar" (John 19:12).

So when Pilate heard these words, he brought Jesus out and sat down on the judgment seat at a place called The Stone Pavement, and in

Aramaic Gabbatha. Now it was the day of Preparation of the Passover. It was about the sixth hour. He said to the Jews, "Behold your King!" They cried out, "Away with him, away with him, crucify him!" Pilate said to them, "Shall I crucify your King?" The chief priests answered, "We have no king but Caesar." So he delivered him over to them to be crucified (John 19:13-16).

Pilate also wrote an inscription and put it on the cross, "Jesus of Nazareth, the King of the Jews" (19:19).

The chief priests of the Jews said to Pilate, "Do not write, 'The King of the Jews,' but rather, 'This man said, I am King of the Jews.'"

Pilate answered, 'What I have written I have written'" (19:21, 22).

John's emphasis on Jesus being a king is clear.

THE REALITY OF JESUS' REIGN

Peter ended his sermon on the Day of Pentecost by declaring,

Let all the house of Israel therefore know for certain that God has made him both Lord and Christ, this Jesus whom you crucified (Acts 2:37).

After His resurrection, Jesus appeared to people on a variety of occasions. On one of those occasions He commissioned His apostles. He declared that "all authority in heaven and on earth..." had been given to Him, and based on that authority He sent them into the whole world to make disciples of all the nations (Matthew 28:18-20; Mark 16:15, 16).

When people are delivered from the power of darkness they are translated into the kingdom of the Son of God's love (Colossians 1:13).

John writes, "The kingdoms of this world have become the kingdom of our Lord and of His Christ, and He shall reign forever and ever!" (Revelation 11:15). He declares that Jesus is Lord of lords and King of kings (17:14).

God ruled, reigned, and protected Israel like no other nation, but Israel rejected Him from being King. So, God gave them a king: first, Saul, then David, then Solomon. At the death of Solomon, the nation of Israel divided into two parts, creating the Northern kingdom and the Southern kingdom. The Northern kingdom was not blessed with a single good king. The Southern kingdom had a few good kings, but not a handful. Israel made a huge mistake in rejecting God from being King.

In spite of it all, the Lord sent His Son to rule over heaven and earth. Let us give thanks.

CHAPTER SEVEN
THE GLORY DEPARTS

Act 1: The Creation
Act 2: The Fall
Act 3: The Story of Israel
    God's Promise to Abraham
    The Giving of the Law
    "Give Us a King" (Part 1)
    "Give Us a King" (Part 2)
    The Glory Departs
    Return from Captivity
    Second Temple Judaism
Act 4: The Story of Jesus
Act 5: The Story of the Church
Act 6: The Return of the King

Israel asked for a king. Their request was a rejection of God as King. God gave them a king—lots of kings. The two books in the Old Testament titled 1 & 2 Kings chronicles the history of Israel under her kings. This part of the Story ends like a nightmare.

Dan Owen has observed that the first eight chapters of 1

Kings begin by describing King Solomon and the glory of his reign and kingdom. Second Kings ends with King Zedekiah being led to Babylon in chains, his eyes gouged out, but only after watching his sons being killed.

The problem with Israel during the time of the kings was the kings. That is the message of 1 & 2 Kings. Under their leadership, Israel became so corrupt that "there was no remedy" (2 Chronicles 36:16). Micah wrote, "her wound is incurable" (1:9). So, God stirred up Nebuchadnezzar, King of Babylon, to destroy Jerusalem. Three sieges were laid against Jerusalem: one in 606 B.C., another in 597 B.C. and a third in 586 B.C.

Ezekiel, a priest of God and prisoner of war in Babylon, sat by the Chebar canal when the hand of the LORD came upon him (Ezekiel 1:3). There, he received a host of visions, one of which signals another turning point in the Story of the Bible.

The vision begins in chapter 8 and ends with chapter 10. He sees something very much like the vision described in the first chapter. (Compare chapter one with chapter 10:20-22.) What he sees is complex. If I were an artist, I would find it difficult to draw what he describes. He sees wheels, four cheribum, and movement. The cheribum have bodies and wings. Each one has four faces: the face of a cherub, the face of a man, the face was of a lion, and the face of an eagle.

Though difficult to conceptualize, we are not left to wonder about the identity of the vision. It is "the glory of the LORD" (Ezekiel 1:28), and Ezekiel sees it making its departure out of the Temple. The glory of the LORD departs!

ICHABOD

Hugh Shira was a man whose preaching first introduced me to
the gospel. I distinctly recall him preaching a sermon on
Ichabod, from 1 Samuel 4. Aside from the title, the only other
part of the sermon I recall had to do with the glory of the Lord
departing. I have read the story a few times since, but for the
longest time, did not understand the reason for the drama it
created in the lives of those mentioned: Eli, Israel, and Eli's
daughter-in-law. My inability to comprehend the drama of this
episode was due to my inability to understand the significance
of the Ark of the Covenant, and not having a comprehensive
picture of the Story of the Bible as a whole.

One point I failed to see was the significance of the presence
of the Lord in Israel. So, let's trace God's presence in the Story
of the Bible.

Readers first see God with man in the Garden of Eden.
After the Fall, there are cameo appearances—visitations with
people like Noah, Abraham, Isaac, Jacob, and Moses. The next
time we read of the LORD abiding with His people is at the
completion of the Tabernacle. God makes His presence known
constantly by means of the pillar of fire and the pillar of cloud.
The movement of the pillar indicated that Israel needed to pack
up and move until the pillar stopped (Exodus 13:17-22).

There were a number of significant items in the Tabernacle,
one being the Ark of the Covenant. After describing the Ark
(Exodus 25:10-22), the LORD says to Moses, "There I will meet
with you, and from above the mercy seat, from between the
two cherubim that are on the ark of the testimony, I will speak
with you about all that I will give you in commandment for the

people of Israel" (25:22). The Ark of the Covenant was placed within the Holy of Holies in the Tabernacle. It was into the Holy of Holies that the high priest would enter once a year (Hebrews 9:1-10).

The Temple Solomon built replaced the Tabernacle. The day Solomon dedicated the Temple,

> ...the priests came out of the Holy place, a cloud filled the house of the LORD, so that the priests could not stand to minister because of the cloud, for the glory of the LORD filled the house of the LORD" (1 Kings 8:10, 11).

Again, the Lord makes His presence known in the place built for Him.

The Ark of the Covenant was, in some sense, connected to the presence of God. This was so much the case that even surrounding nations looked at the Ark of the Covenant as Israel's talisman. They viewed the Ark as the source of Israel's Power, so they stole it.

For Israel, it was the place where the Power met them. It was not the Power itself. But the glory of the LORD was considered by Israel to manifest itself at the Ark. So, the removal of the Ark was equated with the departure of the glory of Israel, YHWH Himself.

When Eli hears of the death of his sons and the theft of the Ark, it was news more than he could bear in his old age. He falls down, breaks his neck, and dies. I do not want to make more of this than should be made, but the text makes it clear that "as soon as he mentioned the ark of God, Eli fell over backward from his seat by the side of the gate, and his neck was broken and he died, for the man was old and heavy" (4:18). It is at the news of the Ark being stolen that he falls and dies.

Eli's daughter-in-law names her child, Ichabod, saying, "The glory has departed from Israel." She says, "The glory has departed from Israel, for the ark of God has been captured." Notice the connection between the glory departing and the ark being captured—and the emphasis on this throughout the text. The departure of the Lord was a traumatic event.

THE DEPARTURE OF THE LORD

The story in 1 Samuel is not the only time the Lord's presence was removed. After partaking of the fruit of the tree of the knowledge of good and evil, Adam and Eve were driven out of the Garden. As you continue reading the following chapters of Genesis, it is not hard to detect that God no longer walked with the first human pair the way He did prior to the Fall.

Then, there is the story we rehearsed from 1 Samuel 4. At one point, the Ark is with Israel. Then, it is captured. Its absence is equated with the departure of the glory of Israel, the glory of God.

Then, there is the departure of God from Israel when Israel and Judah no longer served the true and living God exclusively. They became so corrupt and indistinguishable from their pagan neighbors that they were without remedy (2 Chronicles 36:16). They were taken from the Promised Land into captivity, and the glory of Israel departs, "Then the glory of the LORD went out from the threshold of the house…" (Ezekiel 10:18).

The presence of God seems consistently to convey the idea

of life, strength, grace, hope, love, fellowship, and help. If this is true, then the absence of the Lord would convey the idea of death, abandonment, condemnation, hopelessness, wrath, indignation, and helplessness. It was this kind of condition that knocked Eli off his seat.

The departure of God from Israel is one of the major turning points in Israel's history.

RETURN FROM CAPTIVITY

The Jews of Jesus' day made a number of absurd statements in their discourses with Him. John 8 records one of them. Jesus said, "If you abide in my word, you are truly my disciples, and you will know the truth, and the truth will set you free" (John 8:31, 32).

They answered him, "We are offspring of Abraham and have never been enslaved to anyone. How is it that you say, 'you will become free?'"

How could they say they had never been enslaved to anyone when they were enslaved in Egypt for over 400 years. Every Passover reminded them of their deliverance from bondage.

What about the 70 years they spent in Babylon, not to mention the fact that the sting of Babylonian exile endured through the rule of the Medes and Persians, the Greeks and, at the time of this discussion with Jesus, they were oppressed by the Roman Empire?

Israel's bondage in Egypt was during their formative years as a nation. They were like the proverbial frog in the kettle. They came to Egypt under the duress of a famine. They were received well in Egypt because of Joseph, but a Pharaoh who knew not Joseph arose, and things went bad from there. They dwelt in Egypt as slaves for over 400 years.

Centuries later, due to their rebellion against the law of God and idolatry, Israel was taken from the Promised Land (Deuteronomy 28). In 722 BC, the Assyrians devastated the Northern ten tribes. In 606, 597, and 586 BC, Babylon devastated the Southern two tribes. In 587 BC, the Temple was destroyed.

When the glory of the Lord left the Temple, Israel's source of protection departed. In captivity, they reflected on their situation and its causes. These reflections are recorded in books like Daniel, Ezekiel, and in some of the Psalms. They repented and God opened the door for their return home.

HAPPILY EVER AFTER?

A play written by Stephen Sondheim and a book by James

Lapine titled, *Into the Woods* weaves together four of the Brothers Grimm fairy tales: *Little Red Riding Hood*, *Jack and the Beanstalk*, *Rapunzel*, and *Cinderella*. The first half of the play retells each story. The second half of the play takes these stories beyond their original ending to explore further consequences of the choices of the main characters. The "appendix" to each story explores the imaginative consequences that befell each character who succumbed to the temptation to go *into the woods*. The point made by the play is that in the original telling of the stories everyone lives happily ever after, having learned their lessons, or having obtained the object of their desire. The play suggests that there is more to each story, or, at least, there should have been more.

One would think that Israel's return from captivity would be a nice place to say "…and Israel lived happily ever after"— but it would not be true.

CHALLENGES

All you need to do is read the post-exilic writings of the Old Testament to become familiar with the challenges Israel faced when she returned home. The books of Ezra, Nehemiah, Esther, Haggai, Zechariah, and Malachi reflect that story. Her return to the Promised Land was not her "ending," and it was not "happy."

Ezra

Ezra was a ready scribe (7:6) who "set his heart to study the Law of the Lord, and to do it and to teach his statutes and rules in Israel" (Ezra 7:10). Before the exile, a scribe was little more than a secretary. After the Exile, when prophets became less prominent, and the law of God was being restored, the office of a scribe increased in importance. Ezra was not only a preserver of God's law. He was an interpreter of it.

He lived during Israel's captivity in Babylon, but was also among the ones permitted to return home. The Temple had already been built through the leadership of Zerubbabel. The people had a house for God, but not a heart for God. Ezra's work was to stir up the hearts of Israelites. That they did not have a heart for God is an indicator that Israel's captivity did not end "happy."

Nehemiah

Nehemiah was a cupbearer to the king of Persia, Artaxerxes (2:1). His brother informed him of the captives who had returned to Jerusalem and the condition of that city,

> The remnant that are left of the captivity there in the province are in great affliction and reproach; the wall of Jerusalem also is broken down, and the gates are burned with fire (1:3).

When he heard these words he, "...sat and wept and mourned certain days; and [he] fasted and prayed before the God of heaven" (1:4).

Nehemiah obtained permission from the King of Persia to return to Jerusalem to rebuild the wall. The wall was twelve feet wide, two and one-eighth miles long, and thirty-five feet high. The cupbearer writes, "So we built the wall. And all the wall was joined together to half its height, for the people had a mind to work" (4:6).

While Ezra was rebuilding hearts, Nehemiah was rebuilding the wall.

Esther

In a word, Esther, and cousin, Mordecai, rescue the nation of Israel from genocide.

Haggai

As you can imagine, these books overlap a great deal because the authors are contemporaries. Jerusalem fell in three stages, and as former prisoners-of-war they returned in three stages. Sheshbazzar led the first wave of about 50,000 to Jerusalem in 536 BC (Ezra 2). Ezra led the second group of 2,057 home (Ezra 8). In 445 BC Nehemiah returns with the third group.

It was about 16 years after the first of the exiles returned home that Haggai delivered his message (520 BC). The foundation of the temple was laid, but there it remained untouched for about 16 years. The remnant in that first wave to return home were saying, "It is not the time for us to come, the time for the Lord's house to be built" (Haggai 1:2).

Haggai responded, "Is it a time for you yourselves to dwell in your ceiled houses, while this house lies waste?" (1:4). In other words, the problem is not in times and conditions, but in their hearts.

Hobart Freeman writes,

> They had deluded themselves into believing that if they first made themselves prosperous and satisfied their own needs, they would be in

a better position to meet their obligations to the Lord. What they failed to see, however, was when one neglects to discharge his obligations to the Lord first, whatever he does for himself will not prosper (326).

Haggai's message is, "Consider your ways:"

You have sown much, and harvested little. You eat, but you never have enough; you drink, but you never have your fill. You clothe yourselves, but no one is warm. And he who earns wages does so to put them into a bag with holes (1:6).

Four messages make up the book of Haggai. In essence, they can be summed up by these exhortations: Be involved (in rebuilding the Temple). Be courageous and strong and fearless. Be pure. Be glad.

Zechariah

Some have characterized Zechariah as the apocalypse of the Old Testament due to the number of fantastic visions the prophet receives. It begins with God expressing His displeasure with these post-exilic Israelites, and a call to repentance (1:1-6). God reminds them of His displeasure with Israel of old and that He was faithful to his warnings. In other words, God means what He says and makes no idle threats, "Your fathers, where are they? And the prophets, do they live forever? But my words and my statutes, which I commanded my servants the prophets, did they not overtake our fathers" (1:5, 6a).

The problems Israel faced when they returned home from captivity include the following. They were troubled by the

Samaritans. They were exhausted from the demands that hard labor made on their bodies. Everyone was more interested in their own work, and the building of their own houses than in the rebuilding of the temple. So, rebuilding ceased.

Zechariah lends his voice to Haggai's, urging Israel to complete the building of the Temple.

Malachi

Israel entertained doubts about God's love for His people. Their questions revealed more about them than they would have probably cared to reveal. The questions they asked create a natural outline for the book:

> The LORD said, "I have loved you," but Israel asks, "How have you loved us?" (1:2)

> The Lord asked the people where their honor and fear for Him was. He accused the priests of despising His name. But they said, "How have we despised your name?" (1:6)

> The Lord said they had despised Him by offering polluted food on His altar, but they said, "How have we polluted you?" (1:7). They offered to the Lord things they would not have offered their governor.

> The Lord accuses Israel of being faithless and of having committed abominations. They profaned the sanctuary of the Lord and married the daughter of a foreign god. Their implied question is, "How have we profaned the covenant?" The answer is, "in many ways."

> Malachi accuses Israel of having wearied the Lord with their words, but they say, "How have we wearied him?" Israel wearied the Lord by saying, "Everyone who does evil is good in the sight of the Lord,

and he delights in them," or by saying, "Where is the God of justice?" (2:17).

The Lord pleads with them to return to Him, but they ask, "How shall we return?" The Lord says, "Will man rob God? Yet you are robbing me. But they said, "How have we robbed you?" He answers, "In your tithes and contributions. You are cursed with a curse, for you are robbing me, the whole nation of you." (3:7ff).

Finally, the Lord says, "Your words have been hard against me. They said, "How have we spoken against you?" They went so far as to say "It is vain to serve God. What is the profit of our keeping his charge or of walking as in mourning before the LORD of hosts? And now we call the arrogant blessed. Evildoers not only prosper but they put God to the test and they escape" (3:13-15).

Israel returned from captivity, and lived happily ever after? Hardly.

CHAPTER NINE

SECOND TEMPLE JUDAISM

Act 1: The Creation
Act 2: The Fall
Act 3: The Story of Israel
    God's Promise to Abraham
    The Giving of the Law
    "Give Us a King" (Part 1)
    "Give Us a King" (Part 2)
    The Glory of the Lord Departs
    Return from Captivity
    Second Temple Judaism
Act 4: The Story of Jesus
Act 5: The Story of the Church
Act 6: The Return of the King

(Editorial Note: This chapter borrows so much from N. T. Wright's books, *The New Testament and the People of God*, and *The Challenge of Jesus*, that I must acknowledge little as being my own intellectual property. The reader should consider this chapter as an abstract of these two very useful works.)

Imagine you are walking alongside a building and approaching the corner of an intersection. As you approach the corner, a shadow is cast by someone coming from the other side of the building. You know it is a person by the shadow, but there are a host of things you cannot know because you do not see the person that is casting the shadow. You cannot know the color of their eyes, the color of their hair, their height, their weight, etc.

The four hundred year period of time that lapses between the Old Testament narrative and the New Testament narrative is called by some the *Inter-Testamental* period. An event occurs in this period that casts a shadow on the First Century world. The event is not mentioned explicitly in the Old or New Testament, but it serves as background for understanding the expectations of the Jews you read about in the Gospel accounts.

This event may not be a major turning point in the same way other events mentioned in this book are, but it is important because it helps readers of the New Testament come to terms with the expectations of the Jews when Jesus enters the picture. It also helps the reader to understand the origin of special groups who appear without warning in the New Testament: the Sadducees, the Pharisees, the Essenes, the Herodians.

In this chapter, I will rehearse the story that casts its shadow on the first century, and then I will show how it affected the expectations of Jews of the First Century *Anno Domini*.

HANUKKAH

In the last chapter, we considered the period of time known as the post-exilic period—the period of time that begins with the decree of the Persian King, Cyrus, for the children of Israel to return home after 70 years of Babylonian captivity. The walls and Temple of Jerusalem have been rebuilt. For many scholars today, this period of time is called "Second-Temple Judaism." N. T. Wright comments, "The story of second-temple Judaism is one of tension and tragedy (1992, p. 157)."

The Babylonians destroyed the first Temple in 587 B.C. When the Temple was destroyed Israel faced mounting tension between the faith they professed and the facts they perceived. Babylonian exile not only uprooted them from their land, it placed a big question mark on the faith they placed in the Lord prior to exile. When Babylon was destroyed, and the great moment of their release finally came, Israel was not yet free. The Persians, who crushed Babylon, were generous overlords to the Jews, but still overlords. Alexander the Great swept through the old Persian empire and beyond, painting the political map a new color, and imposing a new culture.

There were two more overlords: Egypt in the third century, and Syria, in the second century, making the story even more complex. This does not alter the fact that the world was now Greek.

> By the time of the first century, if Jesus had wanted to take his disciples to see Euripides' plays performed, he might have openly had to walk down the road from Capernaum to Beth Shean. When Paul was kept prisoner in Caesarea Maritim, he would probably have been able to hear, from his prison cell, the shouts of the crowd in the large amphitheatre, or the applause of the audience in the theatre beside the shore. Nearby there was also a temple to Caesar, a Mithraeum, and probably shrines to other pagan gods.

Herod had shrewdly made the town a bottleneck through which the major trade routes had to pass (Wright 157, 1992).

The Hellenistic cultural setting formed a perpetual cultural and religious threat to the Jews, every bit as powerful as the political one. It was more cerebral than it was visual. Professor Wright states,

> The self-understanding of the Jews at this time was determined by the pressing question as to whether they should attempt to be distinct from this alien culture, and if so how. Pressure to assimilate was strong in many quarters, as is suggested by the evidence of Jews attempting to remove the marks of circumcision (ibid. 158).

The question of identity was forced on Palestinian Jews in a variety of ways, but it was under Syrian rule that the turning point took place which became dangerously determinative for how the Jews understood themselves.

In the second century, a megalomaniac Syrian ruler by the name of Antiochus Epiphanes wanted to use Judaea as a buffer state against Egypt. He tried to gain Jewish support through the high priest, Menelaus, a man who usurped his position.

When the Jews reacted against Menelaus, Antiochus attempted to obtain their loyalty by changing the function and direction of their central religious symbol, the Temple. Antiochus wanted them to think independently, and to service him.

He took control of the Temple on December 25, 167 B.C. He desecrated it so that the Jews would no longer think of it as the place where they were reaffirmed as a unique people. He tried to get the people to worship him. In the ancient world, such a move usually worked quite well. However, Antiochus had not reckoned on the firm monotheistic faith of the Jews.

Some died rather than submit. They believed that God would vindicate His Own name in His chosen place, and His holy law. People who believe this sort of thing tend to act with desperate daring.

A man named Judas Maccabaeus and his companions accomplished the unthinkable. He organized a guerrilla revolt that drove Antiochus Epiphanes out of town. Three years later to the day after the Temple's desecration (Dec. 25, 164 B.C.), Judas cleansed and reconsecrated the temple. A new festival was added to the Jewish calendar called Hanukkah.

The Maccabaean revolt became formative in the same way the Exodus and other great events of Israel's history were. It powerfully reinforced the basic Jewish worldview: when the tyrants rage, the One who dwells in heaven will laugh them to scorn (Psalm 2).

In the years that followed, priest-kings would rule Israel. While this did not dim the sense of the victory of their God, it created the same sort of puzzle that was left after the so-called "return from exile." By no means were all Jews happy with the new situation. Getting rid of the tyrant and his idolatrous practices was one thing, but they were not sure the new form of rule was what God wanted.

The problem was as follows. Judaism was heavily compromised with Hellenism. It overwhelmed some of the religious sensibilities of the Jewish people by, for example, combining the offices of king and high priest. Some opposed it bitterly and set up alternative communities (Essenes). Some remained, but grumbled and tried to reform Israel from within (Pharisees). Others played the power game to win (Sadducees). Most Jews struggled to maintain their livelihood, their loyalty, and their allegiance to national and cultural symbols under the social pressures of warring theologies.

This is the world into which Jesus was born and Paul preached. It explains the appearance of the various sects among the Jews in the New Testament.

DIVERSITY AMONG THE JEWS

> The period between the Babylonian exile and the destruction of the second Temple by the Romans saw the birth of a fascinating and complex variety of expressions of Jewish identity and life. The event which precipitated all the major trends in first-century Judaism was…the Maccabaean crisis (Wright 167, 1992).

Two effects are closely related. The first is the annual celebration of Hanukkah. It kept the triumph of the little band of rebels against the might of paganism before the public eye, which renewed enthusiasm for liberation.

The second is the Maccabaean crisis. It was the cause of the divisions within Judaism, leading to the formation of the Sadducees, the Pharisees, the Essenes, etc.

> How and when Israel's god would rescue his people were questions whose answers, in reflecting different perceptions of what it meant to be the people of the covenant god, divided one

Jewish group from another (Wright, 1992, p. 167).

But the most pressing need of most Jews of the period had
to do with liberation from oppression, from debt, and from
Rome. The hope of Israel, and of most special-interest groups
within Israel, was not for after-death bliss, but for a national
liberation that would fulfill the expectations aroused by the
memory and regular celebration of the Exodus, and nearer at
hand, of the Maccabaean victory. Hope focused on the coming
of the kingdom of Israel's God.

MOVEMENTS OF REVOLT

The books of Maccabees provide the history of the origin of a
number of movements that sought to overthrow oppression,
and bring about the divinely intended kingdom of Israel.
Fidelity to Torah, readiness for martyrdom, resistance to
compromise, and resolute military action, that was the
combination that would win the day. How very different this is
to the way liberation was actually accomplished through Jesus.

Movements arose in whose eyes Jerusalem was the center of
a corrupt and illicit regime. For example, the Essenes refused
to have anything to do with the "cleansed" Temple, and
established their own community elsewhere. They proclaimed
by their very mode of existence that though they longed for the
liberation of Israel they were simply going to wait and allow
Israel's God to bring it to pass in His own time.

The Pharisees worked with the system. They believed that
Israel's God would act; but loyal Jews may well be required as
the agents and instruments of that divine action.

The Sadducees proclaimed by their very existence that they believed in seizing and maintaining political power for themselves.

These political movements represent three options. Though the Essenes were a religious group, they did not distinguish between religion and politics. They were a community of people who made a place for themselves on the North East of the Dead Sea at Qumran. They separated themselves from the wicked world, and waited for God to do whatever God was going to do.

The second option was the compromise option taken by Herod: build yourself fortresses and palaces, get along with your political bosses as well as you can, do as well as you can, and hope that God will validate it somehow (p. 37, *The Challenge of Jesus*).

The third option was the zealot option, that of the Sicarri, "The Dagger Men." They overtook Herod's old palace and the fortress of Masada during the Roman/Jewish war. N. T. Wright characterizes their mentality:

> Say your prayers, sharpen your swords, make yourselves holy to fight a holy war, and God will give you a military victory that will also be the theological victory of good over evil, of God over the hordes of darkness, of the Son of Man over the monsters" (1999, p. 37).

It is only when we see Jesus in the context of His day that we begin to realize how striking and dramatic His agenda and His life was. He was neither a quietist (pacifist), nor a compromiser, nor a zealot. He went back to Israel's Scriptures and recalled another kingdom model.

The Gospel accounts (Matthew, Mark, Luke, and John) begin with the proclamation, "The kingdom of God is at hand." God is now unveiling His age-old plan, bringing His sovereignty to bear on Israel and the world as He had always intended, bringing justice and mercy to Israel and the world. And He did so through Jesus.

CHAPTER TEN

THE STORY OF JESUS

Act 1: The Creation
Act 2: The Fall
Act 3: The Story of Israel
    God's Promise to Abraham
    The Giving of the Law
    "Give Us a King" (Part 1)
    "Give Us a King" (Part 2)
    The Glory of the Lord Departs
    Return from Captivity
    Second Temple Judaism
Act 4: The Story of Jesus
Act 5: The Story of the Church
Act 6: The Return of the King

If the phrase had not long ago been reduced to a cliché, "Jesus Saves" would serve admirably as an adequate summary for what our Scriptures have to say on the subject. But bumper stickers and graffiti have isolated the phrase so completely from the story to which it is the punch line that all the meaning has been drained out of the words. We need to recover the salvation *story* if the salvation *words* are to mean anything. Salvation is not a one-night stand. It cannot be isolated from the thick texture of history; it is all-encompassing, pulling everything that has happened and happens, and every person named and unnamed, into relationship with the work of God in history (Peterson 2005, p. 147).

"'The gospel' is God's good news, promised long ago, about his dying and rising son, the Messiah, the lord of the world. When this message is announced, things happen: (a) the creator God is shown to be 'in the right' in that he has kept his promises, (b) people of all sorts, Jew and Greek alike, receive 'salvation' as a result of the divine power, (c) Paul is not ashamed (as he might have been, announcing a message which he knew to be folly to Greeks and a scandal to Jews), and (d) he is the more eager to preach the same message anywhere and everywhere, not least right under Caesar's nose in Rome." (Wright, 2013, p. 916-917).

A good place for us to begin this chapter is with one of the many appearances Jesus made after His resurrection from the dead. He appeared to two disciples who were making there way to Emmaus, a city about seven miles from Jerusalem (Luke 24:13). Luke writes, "but their eyes were kept from recognizing him" (24:16). The only thing these two disciples knew was that Jesus was

a man who was a prophet mighty in deed and word before God and all the people, and how (their) chief priests and rulers delivered him up to be condemned to death, and crucified him (Luke 24:19-20).

Then, they said, "but we had hoped that he was the one to redeem Israel." They heard reports concerning the empty tomb, but apparently did not know what to make of them.

Jesus, unrecognized by these two men, said,

'Was it not necessary that the Christ should suffer these things and enter into his glory?' and beginning with Moses and all the Prophets, he interpreted to them in all the Scriptures the things concerning himself (Luke 24:26, 28).

Jesus, still unrecognized by the two, remained with them for bread at their request. When Jesus broke the bread and gave it to them, Luke writes, "And their eyes were opened, and they recognized him. And he vanished from their sight" (Luke 24:31).

They said to one another, "Did not our hearts burn within us while he talked to us on the road, while he opened to us the Scriptures?" Then they returned to Jerusalem to report what had just taken place (Luke 24:36-53).

When Jesus was with the two disciples on the road to Emmaus, he reminded them saying, "Was it not necessary that the Christ should suffer these things and enter into his glory?" (Luke 24:26). To the eleven and those with them, He said,

these are my words that I spoke to you while I was still with you, that everything written about me in the Law of Moses and the Prophets and the Psalms must be fulfilled" (Luke 24:44).

The Old Testament spoke about the Coming One. He came—that's the middle of the story. And he's coming again— that's the end of the story.

THE MIDDLE OF THE STORY

A summary of the birth, life, death, resurrection, and coronation of Christ can be found in a single verse—Revelation 12:5. The woman described in Revelation 12 gives birth to a child. The red dragon is standing before the woman to devour the child when he is born. John writes, "she gave birth to a male child, one who is to rule all the nations with a rod of iron, but her child was caught up to God and to his throne…" (12:5).

A sketch of Jesus' life might look something like the following. He:

…was born of a virgin and begotten by God (Matt 1)

…increased in wisdom and stature and in favor with God and man (Lk 2:52).

…was baptized of John "to fulfill all righteousness" (Matt 3:13ff).

…was a man approved of God unto you by mighty works and wonders and signs which God did by him… (Acts 2:22).

…was delivered up by the determinate counsel and foreknowledge of God, and crucified by the hand of lawless men (Acts 2:23).

…but God raised Him up, having loosed the pangs of death: because it was not possible that he should be holden of it (Acts 2:24).

…was changed: his flesh did not see corruption (Acts 2:24-32).

…ascended into heaven and was seated at the right hand of God exalted (Acts 2:33, 34).

…was made both Lord and Christ (Acts 2:36).

The emphasis in all four gospel accounts is on the last week of His life. All four authors slow down the pace of their storytelling to the last week. Matthew sets out to identify Jesus as the promised Messiah. Many have argued that his primary audience was the Jews of his day. The last twenty-nine percent of his story focuses on the last week of Jesus' life—his entry into Jerusalem, death, burial and resurrection. (All percentages are taken from Leland Ryken's book, *Words of Delight*, p. 382).

Mark focuses the reader's attention on the power of Christ. Most commentators agree that he probably wrote appealing to Roman citizen. The last thirty-eight percent of his account centers on the last week.

Luke writes with the clear intention of appealing to the Gentiles. The last twenty-five percent of his account puts the literary magnifying glass on the events of the last week.

John's appeal is to mankind in general and emphasizes the deity of Christ. Thirty-eight percent of his account concerns the last week.

Leland Ryken, professor of literature at Wheaton College, writes,

> Increasing specificity of detail characterizes the storytelling method as the writers reach the passion account. Obviously this is what the Gospel writers regarded as most important in their stories" (1992, p. 382).

Scot McKnight affirms that all four Gospel accounts, "… focus on the death and resurrection of the hero—Jesus—more than any story in ancient history" (2011, p. 82).

Consider also the emphasis on Jesus' death, burial, and

resurrection in some of the sermons recorded in the book of Acts. The majority of the sermon Peter preached on Pentecost (Acts 2:22-36) focuses on this event. Peter preached the resurrection of Christ to Cornelius (Acts 10:39ff). We can see the same emphasis in other sermons as well: Acts 3:11-26; 4:1-12; 10:34-43; 13:26-41.

The people in Athens initially thought that Paul was a, "setter forth of strange gods because he preached Jesus and the resurrection" (Acts 17:18). Because his teachings were new, they were willing to listen. Luke comments parenthetically, "Now all the Athenians and the strangers sojourning there spent their time in nothing else but either to tell or to hear some new thing." When they heard the message of the resurrection of the dead, some mocked; but others said, "We will hear you again about this" (Acts 17:32). (The disciples of Jesus and the disciples of Socrates meet for the first time.)

When Paul was in Jerusalem, he delivered a public message to a mob of people who were out to murder him. In that message, he recounts the story of his conversion, which includes his confrontation with the resurrected Christ on the road to Damascus. When he was standing before the Jerusalem council, he pitted the Sadducees and Pharisees against one another when he said, "Brothers, I am a Pharisee, a son of Pharisees. It is with respect to the hope and the resurrection of the dead that I am on trial" (Acts 23:6).

When he stood before Felix, the governor, he informed him that he was on trial for,

> believing all things which are according to the law, and which are

written in the prophets; having hope toward God, which these also themselves look for, that there shall be a resurrection both of the just and unjust (Acts 24:14f).

You cannot escape the subject in the New Testament— whether it is a reference to the resurrection of Jesus Christ, our Lord, or a reference to the subject of the resurrection, which instills us with hope. Jesus is our hope.

"According to his great mercy, he has caused us to be born again to a living hope through the resurrection of Jesus Christ from the dead" (1 Peter 1:3).

The hope for which we are to stand ready to give an answer centers on Jesus' resurrection from the dead (1 Peter 3:15).

Paul devotes a tremendous amount of ink on the subject as recorded in 1 Corinthians 15. The first few verses tell us that the death, burial, resurrection, and appearances of Christ are the good news, the gospel.

Paul argues that not only was Jesus raised, but that He was raised for our justification (Romans 4:25). No resurrection/no justification.

When we are baptized into Christ we re-enact the gospel:

How can we who died to sin still live in it? Do you not know that all of us who have been baptized into Christ Jesus were baptized into his death? We were buried therefore with him by baptism into death, in order that, just as Christ was raised from the dead by the glory of the Father, we too might walk in newness of life" (Romans 6:2-4).

The sampling of texts above do not begin to touch the

plethora of references on this subject in the New Testament.

C. S. Lewis wrote an essay titled, "The Grand Miracle." He begins the essay writing,

> One is very often asked at present whether we could not have a Christianity stripped, or, as people who ask it say, "freed" from its miraculous elements, a Christianity with the miraculous elements suppressed. Now, it seems to me that precisely the one religion in the world, or, at least, the only one I know, with which you could not do that is Christianity (2000, p. 3).

The essence of other religions would not be affected if you removed the miraculous elements of their stories. In fact, Mr. Lewis argues, they may even be enhanced because the miracles of these stories "largely contradict the teaching."

"But," he writes,

> ...you cannot possibly do that with Christianity, because the Christian story is precisely the story of one grand miracle, the Christian assertion being that what is beyond all space and time, what is uncreated, eternal, came into nature, into human nature, descended into His own universe, and rose again, bringing nature up with him. It is precisely one great miracle. If you take that away there is nothing specifically Christian left (Lewis, 2000, p. 4).

As he develops his argument, Mr. Lewis asks us to imagine finding a manuscript of some great work, either of a symphony or a novel. Someone else comes to us and says,

> Here is a new bit of the manuscript that I found; it is the central passage of that symphony, or the central chapter of that novel. The

text is incomplete without it. I have got the missing passage which is really the centre of the whole work (p. 4).

The only thing you could do is place the passage in the middle of the essay to see how it reacts with the rest of the manuscript.

If it constantly brought out new meanings for the whole of the rest of the work, if it made you notice things in the rest of the work which you had not noticed before, then I think you would decide that it was authentic. On the other hand, if it failed to do that, then, however attractive it was in itself, you would reject it.

Now, what is the missing chapter in this case, the chapter which Christians are offering? The story of the Incarnation is the story of the descent and resurrection... (p. 4)

He concludes the essay in this way,

That is why I think this Grand Miracle is the missing chapter in this novel, the chapter on which the whole plot turns; that is why I believe that God really has dived down into the bottom of creation, and has come up bringing the whole redeemed nature on His shoulders (p. 9).

Jesus' resurrection from the dead is one of the major turning points in the Bible. Very little remains untouched by this event. It is Jesus' resurrection from the dead that turned the world upside down—or as one man put it, turned the world right side up.

CHAPTER ELEVEN
THE CHURCH

Act 1: The Creation
Act 2: The Fall
Act 3: The Story of Israel
    God's Promise to Abraham
    The Giving of the Law
    "Give Us a King" (Part 1)
    "Give Us a King" (Part 2)
    The Glory of the Lord Departs
    Return from Captivity
    Second Temple Judaism
Act 4: The Story of Jesus
Act 5: The Story of the Church
Act 6: The Return of the King

God promised Abraham that through his seed all the families of the earth would be blessed (Genesis 12:3). This promise is repeated to Abraham in Genesis 22:18, to Isaac in Genesis 26:1-4, and to Jacob in Gen. 28:14. The promise is ultimately fulfilled in Jesus Christ. Paul offers this inspired commentary,

> Now to Abraham and to his seed were the promises made. He does not say, 'And to seeds,' as of many, but as of one, 'And to your Seed,' who is Christ" (Galatians 3:16).

The blessing is identified explicitly in the second recorded sermon of Peter's in the book of Acts, "God, having raised up his servant, sent him to you first, to bless you by turning every one of you from your wickedness" (Acts 3:26). This is equivalent to repentance and having our sins forgiven.

In the first sermon recorded in Acts, the Spirit of God convicts the Pentecost audience of having murdered the Son of God. Peter argues that Jesus was approved of by God, delivered up by lawless men, crucified and slain, raised from the dead by God, and that he was exalted at the right hand of God (Acts 2:22-36). The audience was pricked in their hearts and said, "Brothers, what shall we do?"

Peter said, "Repent and be baptized every one of you in the name of Jesus Christ for the forgiveness of your sins, and you will receive the gift of the Holy Spirit" (Acts 2:38). Peter was being obedient to the commission given to him by the Lord prior to His ascension (Mark 16:16 Matthew 28:19ff).

The establishment of the church is of tremendous importance in the grand scheme of the Story of the Bible in two ways. First, her establishment fulfills prophecies concerning the reign of God, and second, it is the Temple of God.

FULFILLMENT OF PROPHECY

First of all, the establishment of the church fulfills prophecies concerning the reign of God. Coincidently, many of these prophetic texts appear in the second chapter of the books in which we find them:

Isaiah 2:1-5 (repeated in Micah 4:1-3)

The word that Isaiah the son of Amoz saw concerning Judah and Jerusalem. It shall come to pass in the latter days that the mountain of the house of the LORD shall be established as the highest of the mountains, and shall be lifted up above the hills; and all the nations shall flow to it, and many peoples shall come, and say: "Come let us go up to the mountain of the Lord, to the house of the God of Jacob, that he may teach us his ways and that we may walk in his paths." For out of Zion shall go the law, and the word of the LORD from Jerusalem. He shall judge between the nations, and shall decide disputes for many peoples; and they shall beat their swords into plowshares, and their spears into pruning hooks; nation shall not lift up sword against nation, neither shall they learn war anymore. O house of Jacob, come, let us walk in the light of the LORD."

Daniel 2:36-44

This is the dream. Now we will tell the king its interpretation. You, O king, the king of kings, to whom the God of heaven has given the kingdom, the power, and the might, and the glory, and into whose hand he has given, wherever they dwell, the children of man, the beasts of the field, and the birds of the heavens, make you rule over them all—you are the head of gold. Another kingdom inferior to you shall arise after you, and yet a third kingdom of bronze, which shall rule over all the earth. And there shall be a fourth kingdom, strong as iron, because iron breaks to pieces and shatters all things. And like iron that crushes, it shall break and crush all these. And as you saw the feet and toes, partly of potter's clay and partly of iron, it shall be a divided kingdom, but some of the firmness of iron shall be in it, just as you saw iron mixed with the soft clay. And as the toes of the feet were partly iron and partly clay, so the kingdom shall be partly strong and partly brittle. As you saw the iron mixed with soft clay, so they will mix with one another in marriage, but they will not hold together just as iron does not mix with clay. And in the days of those kings the God of heaven, will set up a kingdom that shall never be destroyed, nor shall the kingdom be left to another people. It shall break in pieces all these kingdoms and bring them to an end, and it shall stand forever, just as you saw that a stone was cut from a mountain by no human hand, and that it broke in pieces the iron, the bronze, the clay, the silver, and the gold. A great God has made known to the king what shall be after this. The dream is certain, and its interpretation sure."

Joel 2:28-32

And it shall come to pass afterward, that I will pour out my Spirit on all flesh; your sons and your daughters shall prophesy, your old men shall dream dreams, and your young men shall see visions. Even on the male and female servants in those days I will pour out my Spirit. And I will show wonders in the heavens and on the earth, blood and fire and columns of smoke. The sun shall be turned to darkness, and the moon to blood, before the great and awesome day of the LORD comes. And it shall come to pass that everyone who calls on the name of the Lord shall be saved. For in Mount Zion and in Jerusalem there shall be those who escape, as the LORD has said, and among the survivors shall be those whom the LORD calls.

On the first Pentecost after the resurrection of Jesus Christ, the apostles were speaking in tongues. They were accused of being drunken. Peter defends them, saying, "For these are not drunken, as you suppose; since it is only the third hour of the day. But this is what was uttered through the prophet Joel." He then quotes Joel 2:28ff.

What transpired on the day of Pentecost is so significant that a professor at Harding University, James D. Bales, wrote a book on this one chapter of Scripture, and titled it, *The Hub of the Bible*. In the Preface of the book, he writes:

> Acts Two is one of the most significant chapters in the Bible. It relates to much that had gone before and it bears some relationship to all that follows after. The events that took place on that day were the fulfillment of promises and predictions which God had made through the prophets and through Jesus Christ in His personal ministry. It not only marks the fulfillment, or the beginning of the fulfillment, of many prophecies but it also marks the beginning of the reign of Jesus as Lord and Christ at God's right hand. Thus it marks the time of the establishment of the church.
>
> The individual who understands the significance of the events that took place on this first Pentecost after the resurrection of Christ, is in a position to understand much of the rest of the Bible. He who does not understand their significance is confused with reference to many other things in the Bible. For these reasons Acts Two may be called *The Hub of the Bible* (4).

On the day of Pentecost Jesus founded His church, purchased with His own blood (Acts 20:28).

The church is referred to, among other metaphors, as the body of Christ. Writers of Scripture place emphasis on there being one body: not one for the Jews and another for the Gentiles (Ephesians 4:4; 1 Cor. 12:13). God "...put all things under his feet and gave him as head over all things to the church, which is his body, the fullness of him who fills all in all" (Ephesians 1:22, 23).

THE CHURCH IS THE TEMPLE OF GOD

Second, the church is the temple in which God dwells today.

There are three main events described in the book of Exodus. The first two are the Exodus (1-8), and the giving of the Law (19-40). The third is the construction of the Tabernacle (Chaps. 35-40). After God describes the tabernacle in detail, Moses tells Israel, "Then you shall erect the tabernacle according to the plan for it that you were shown on the mountain" (Exodus 26:30). Moses delivers to Israel all the details concerning the building of the Tabernacle. Exodus 40:33 records, "So Moses finished the work."

Now notice Exodus 40:34-38,

> Then the cloud covered the tent of meeting, and the glory of Jehovah filled the tabernacle. And Moses was not able to enter into the tent of meeting, because the cloud abode thereon, and the glory of Jehovah filled the tabernacle. And when the cloud was taken up from over the tabernacle, the children of Israel went onward, throughout all their journeys: but if the cloud was not taken up, then they journeyed not till the day that it was taken up. For the cloud of Jehovah was upon the tabernacle by day, and there was fire therein by night, in the sight of all the house of Israel, throughout all their journeys (ASV).

The tent was built and the prescribed furniture was set in place: the table, the ark, the candlestick, etc., (Exodus 40:16-33). Then, it was filled with the glory of the Lord.

Some 500 years later, King David expressed his reluctance, perhaps even embarrassment, that he dwelt in a house of cedar while the ark resided in a tent. However, David was a man who shed much blood. So, building a Temple was left to his son,

Solomon.

> Thus all the work that king Solomon did on the house of the LORD was finished. And Solomon brought in the things that David his father had dedicated, the silver, the gold, and the vessels, and stored them in the treasuries of the house of the LORD (1 Kings 7:51).

Solomon assembled all the men of Israel to a feast to dedicate the Temple. Sacrifices were offered and the Ark of the Covenant was brought into the most holy place and set under the wings of the cherubim (1 Kings 8:1-9). Now notice,

> And when the priests came out of the Holy Place, a cloud filled the house of the LORD, so that the priests could not stand to minister because of the cloud, for the glory of the LORD filled the house of the LORD (1 Kings 8:10).

Rick Oster observes that the Tabernacle and the Temple,

> ...became not just a symbol of God's presence but a space filled with God, a place of Real Presence. God's presence was not confined to the tabernacle but there was an intensity of glory of Presence not true of any other place (Allen, 129, 2001).

On the day of Pentecost another great edifice was built— not one of cloth and poles, or brick and mortar, but one made of " living stones...built up as a spiritual house, to be a holy priesthood, to offer spiritual sacrifices acceptable to God through Jesus Christ" (1 Peter 2:4, 5).

Paul writes, " Do you not know that you are God's temple and that God's Spirit dwells in you?" (1 Corinthians 3:16).

Collectively, the church is the temple of God. Rick Oster writes, "…it follows quite naturally that God's Spirit would dwell in His temple" (Allen 102).

The church of our Lord is inhabited by God's Spirit. The evidence is two-fold: the scriptures affirm it (1 Corinthians 3), and the fruit of her members exhibit it (Gal 5).

The pattern is evident. An edifice—the Tabernacle, the Temple, the church—is erected by God's authority. God indwells the edifice erected for His presence. Evidence of this phenomenon is seen in the glory of the Lord that filled both the Tabernacle and the Temple. Where the church is concerned, the Spirit of God bears fruit, as is evident in changed lives.

There is a fourth edifice built by God that I failed to mention earlier. The fourth is Jesus Christ. John says that He became flesh and dwelt (literally, pitched His tent) among us (John 1:14). In Him dwells all the fullness of the Godhead bodily (Col 2:9).

I affirmed at the onset of this book that God's eternal purpose is to draw all men into the one body of the saved. God inhabits that one body. His presence is, among other things, an earnest of our inheritance (Ephesians 1:13, 14). He saves all men in this one body "to the praise of the glory of His grace" (Ephesians 1:3-14). He calls us through the Gospel (2 Thessalonians 2:14). He calls us to believe, repent, and be baptized in the name of His Son (Matt 28:18ff; Mark 16:16; Acts 2:38), and we are to walk in the light (1 John 1:5-10).

Some have mistakenly treated the church as an afterthought or an "emergency measure" concocted by God on the spur of the moment when His Son was hanged on the cross—when

"Plan A" failed. This is not the image of the church I take away from my reading of the Bible. Paul treats the church as being in the mind of God before the foundation of the world (Ephesians 3:11). It is the kingdom Jesus died to establish. It is the beginning of God's new creation. It is one of the pivotal moments in the Story of the Bible.

CHAPTER TWELVE
THE RETURN OF THE KING

Act 1: The Creation
Act 2: The Fall
Act 3: The Story of Israel
    God's Promise to Abraham
    The Giving of the Law
    "Give Us a King" (Part 1)
    "Give Us a King" (Part 2)
    The Glory of the Lord Departs
    Return from Captivity
    Second Temple Judaism
Act 4: The Story of Jesus
Act 5: The Story of the Church
Act 6: The Return of the King

Some of the Psalms in the Old Testament are called "envelop" Psalms. They begin and end with the same line. Psalm 103 is an example. It begins and ends with the line: "Bless the Lord, O my soul" (Psalm 103:1, 22).

The Story of the Bible has an envelop structure in that it begins and ends on the same themes. It begins with man losing some of the most valuable qualities of his existence, but it ends with the hope of receiving what we, humanity, lost in the beginning.

I asked the reader, at the beginning of our study, to be patient for the very purpose of seeing how studying the biblical narrative is important for the purpose of coming around full circle when we reach the end.

In Chapter One, I wrote,

> The story of the Bible begins with the loss of innocence, the introduction of guilt, a loss of access to immortality, a loss of Eden, and separation from God. For God's family, the story of the Bible ends with access to a river of the water of life, and to the tree of life, forgiveness, and life in the presence of God. The closing chapters of the Bible tell us that we gain the very things we lost in the beginning of the story. The end helps to make sense of the beginning. The beginning finds its significance or fulfillment in the end.

In Genesis 2, Adam walked with God in the garden in the cool of the day. After Genesis 3 (the Fall), God no longer walked with man as he did before the Fall. We get cameo appearances of Him throughout the story. In Jesus, we get a full view of Him.

The last book of the Bible describes a renewal of God's project in creation.

> Then I saw a new heaven and a new earth, for the first heaven and the first earth had passed away, and the sea was no more. And I saw the holy city, new Jerusalem, coming down out of heaven from God, prepared as a bride adorned for her husband. And I heard a loud voice from the throne saying, 'Behold, the dwelling place of God is with

man. He will dwell with them, and they will be his people, and God himself will be with them as their God. He will wipe away every tear from their eyes, and death shall be no more, neither shall there be mourning nor crying nor pain anymore, for the former things have passed away.

And he who was seated on the throne said, 'Behold, I am making all things new.' Also he said, 'Write this down, for these words are trustworthy and true. And he said to me, 'It is done! I am the Alpha and the Omega, the beginning and the end.' (Revelation 21:1-6a).

I want to close our study by tying it in with a recurring theme that runs throughout the entire Bible—that subject being, God is King. He was king before the flood. He was king as he led Israel out of Egypt, through the wilderness, and into the promised land. Israel rejected Him as king, and asked for another. God gave them what they asked for—kings, and more kings. But, God returns as King through His Son, Jesus Christ. Through Jesus' death, burial and resurrection, He ascends to the right hand of the throne of God as King of kings, and Lord of lords. And He will return.

THE RETURN OF THE KING

In the Bible, God appears as a soldier or warrior who asserts His power against the evil in the world. When the Israelites celebrated their deliverance from the Egyptian army on the far side of the sea, they said, "YHWH is a man of war: YHWH is His name" (Exo. 15:3).

The *Dictionary of Biblical Imagery* notes:

Israel and the entire ancient Near East knew almost constant warfare.

Armies were always on the move, either in the interest of expanding imperial territories or defending against foreign encroachment (p. 211).

An image used to depict the second coming of our Lord is a king returning from war:

> Then I saw heaven opened, and behold, a white horse! The one sitting on it is called Faithful and True, and in righteousness he judges and makes war. His eyes are like a flame of fire, and on his head are many diadems, and he has a name written that no one knows but himself. He is clothed in a robe dipped in blood, and the name by which he is called is "The Word of God." And the armies of heaven, arrayed in fine linen, white and pure, were following him on white horses. From his mouth comes a sharp sword with which to strike down the nations, and he will rule them with a rod of iron. He will tread the winepress of the fury of the wrath of God the Almighty. On his robe and on his thigh he has a name written, King of kings and Lord of lords (Revelation 19:11-16).

Some consider this text parallel with Isaiah 63:1-6:

> Who is this who comes from Edom,
> in crimsoned garments from Bozrah,
> he who is splendid in his apparel,
>> marching in the greatness of his strength?
> "It is I, speaking in righteousness,
>> mighty to save."
>
> Why is your apparel red,
>> and your garments like his who treads in the winepress?
>
> "I have trodden the winepress alone,

and from the peoples no one was with me;
I trod them in my anger
and trampled them in my wrath;
their lifeblood spattered on my garments,
and stained all my apparel.
For the day of vengeance was in my heart,
and my year of redemption had come.
I looked, but there was no one to help;
I was appalled, but there was no one to uphold;
so my own arm wrought me salvation,
and my wrath upheld me.
I trampled down the peoples in my anger;
I made them drunk in my wrath,
and I poured out their lifeblood on the earth."

The Lord's garments are drenched with the blood of His enemies. When He returns as our victorious King, His appearance will be heralded by the blast of a trumpet. "The trumpet will sound, and the dead will be raised imperishable and we shall be changed" (1 Corinthians 15:52). He will "descend from heaven with a cry of command, with the voice of an archangel, and with the sound of the trumpet of God" (1 Thessalonians 4:16). As people in the ancient world filed out of the city to meet their victorious king returning home, so we shall all be gathered together for the return of our King. "We who are alive, who are left, will be caught up together with them in the clouds to meet the Lord in the air, and so we will always be with the Lord" (1 Thessalonians 4:17). This will occur when Jesus has put all His enemies under His feet (1 Corinthians 15:25). "The last enemy to be destroyed is death" (15:26).

SUMMARY

The Story of the Bible is all about the salvation of man, through Jesus Christ to the glory of God. All things were created through Jesus Christ to the glory of God (John 1:3; Colossians 1:15-16). The graciousness of God is made evident in the Fall. God could have simply destroyed man, giving him nothing more than he deserved. Due to His graciousness and mercy, He devised a plan to save man. This plan was set before the foundations of the world.

This is where the promise to Abraham comes in. God promised to bless all nations through the seed of Abraham. Paul informs us that the seed God had in mind was Jesus Christ (Galatians 3:16), and the blessing that is extended to all nations is the forgiveness of sins (Acts 3:26).

Then, there is King David. David wanted to build a house for God. However, God said,

> When your days are fulfilled and you lie down with your fathers, I will raise up your offspring after you, who shall come from your body, and I will establish his kingdom. He shall build a house for my name, and I will establish the throne of his kingdom forever (2 Samuel 7:12, 13).

God promised to "establish his offspring forever and his throne as the days of the heavens" (Psalm 89:29). He said,

> I will not remove from him my steadfast love
> or be false to my faithfulness.
> I will not violate my covenant
> or alter the word that went forth from my lips.
> Once for all I have sworn by my holiness:

I will not lie to David.
His offspring shall endure forever,
  his throne as long as the sun before me.
Like the moon it shall be established forever,
  a faithful witness in the skies" (Psalm 89:33-37).

Now, listen to the Apostle Peter, as he reflects on these texts and speaks of King David,

> Being therefore a prophet and knowing that God had sworn with an oath to him that he would set one of his descendants on his throne, he foresaw and spoke about the resurrection of Christ, that he was not abandoned to Hades, nor did his flesh see corruption (Acts 2:30, 31).

Peter goes on to herald the fact that Christ is now seated on David's throne, establishing the fact that the kingdom has begun with Jesus as reigning Lord and Christ.

A well known preacher, Johnny Ramsey, used to say that the Old Testament looks forward to someone coming. The Gospel accounts tell us He is here. The epistles tell us He is coming again.

Peter warned that mockers will come asking, "Where is the promise of His coming?" (2 Peter 3:4).

> For they deliberately overlook this fact, that the heavens existed long ago, and the earth was formed out of water and through water by the word of God, and that by means of these the world that then existed was deluged with water and perished. But by the same word the heavens and earth that now exist are stored up for fire, being kept until the day of judgment and destruction of the ungodly. But do not overlook this one fact, beloved, that with the Lord one day is as a

thousand years, and a thousand years as one day. The Lord is not slow to fulfill his promise as some count slowness, but is patient toward you, not wishing that any should perish, but that all should reach repentance. But the day of the Lord will come like a thief, and then the heavens will pass away with a roar, and the heavenly bodies will be burned up and dissolved, and the earth and the works that are done on it will be exposed. Since all these things are thus to be dissolved, what sort of people ought you to be in lives of holiness and godliness, waiting for and hastening the coming of the day of God, because of which the heavens will be set on fire and dissolved, and the heavenly bodies will melt as they burn! But according to his promise we are waiting for new heavens and a new earth in which righteousness dwells (2 Peter 3:5-13).

WHOSE SIDE ARE YOU ON?

C. S. Lewis' book, *Mere Christianity*, is four smaller books that were put together in one volume. Initially, they were talks he gave over the radio. The second book is titled, *What Christians Believe*. He ends that book, addressing the subject of the return of Christ. He writes,

...we can guess why He is delaying. He wants to give us the chance of joining His side freely. I do not suppose you and I would have thought much of a Frenchman who waited till the Allies were marching into Germany and then announced he was on our side. God will invade. But I wonder whether people who ask God to interfere openly and directly in our world quite realize what it will be like when He does. When that happens, it is the end of the world. When the author walks on to the stage the play is over. God is going to invade, all right: but what is the good of saying you are on His side then, when you see the whole natural universe melting away like a dream and something else—something it never entered your head to conceive—comes crashing in; something so beautiful to some of us and so terrible to others that none of us will have any choice left? For this time it will be God without disguise; something so overwhelming that it will strike either irresistible love or irresistible horror into every creature. It will be too late then to choose your side. There is no use saying you choose to lie down when it has become impossible to stand up. That will not be the time for choosing: it will be the time when we discover which side we really have chosen, whether we realize it before or not. Now, to-day, this moment, is our chance to choose the right side. God is holding back to give us that chance. It will not last forever. We must take it or leave it (65).

This will be the final turning point, the culmination of God's plan of redemption, the goal or aim of the kingdom of God. Who, in their right mind, would choose to be outside God's grace when He comes?

CHAPTER THIRTEEN

BENEFITS

A round five years ago, I presented the material in this book to a retirement home in Upland, CA. One Monday morning, a new resident entered the room just as we were waiting to begin. Some of the residents registered their displeasure when they saw him, and a few whispered something to their neighbor. I thought, *here's trouble*.

I began class by briefly surveying the Story of the Bible by means of the Six Acts. We were ready to begin our study of Act 4: The Story of Jesus.

Our visitor raised his hand, and asked if we were going to discuss Jesus' marriage to Mary Magdalene, and the little girl born of that union, and how the three rushed off to what is now modern day France. The open display of disgust on the faces of some was obvious, but the man was not put off by their contempt. In fact, he seemed to be further fueled by it.

I told him that he raised some interesting issues, but that we would not be discussing them in this class because our explicit purpose was to retell the Story of the Bible, and the particulars he mentioned are no part of that story. I also told him that I would be glad to discuss those sorts of things with him after class, or when we came to a close of our study a month or two later.- He did not stay after class was over to discuss the issues he raised.

Consider the benefit of this approach. Restricting our study to the Story of the Bible allowed us the freedom to politely affirm that the incidents the old gentleman brought up were no part of the Story as told in the Bible, and that our purpose was to study *that* Story.

It is profoundly important that we get *that* Story told first. It has a right to be heard. It protects us from being distracted by theories that circle around it like buzzards waiting to eat the left overs.

There is a time and place for theories and for exploring possibilities, but there is a time for reading or learning the Story as told in the Bible as well. Theories and possibilities can, sometimes, be very distracting.

I would like for you to consider some other benefits.

THE PROBLEM OF EVIL

Consider the problem of evil. The Bible affirms that God is infinite in His power and infinite in His goodness, and yet sin and suffering exist. The atheist debaters of the past few decades affirm that the God of the Bible cannot be both infinite in His goodness and His power because sin and suffering exist. There is an implied, unspoken proposition in their "argument": A God who is infinite in power and goodness would eliminate sin and suffering. But, because sin and suffering exist, God cannot be both infinite in power and goodness. He lacks infiniteness in one or both qualities—they claim.

We usually try to meet the atheist in his own philosophical camp, but who says we must meet him on his own terms? Consider how a knowledge of the narrative of Scripture addresses the issue. The middle of the Story—the account of Jesus's life, death, burial and resurrection—answers the question of whether the God of the Bible addresses the issue of sin and suffering.

Paul affirms that "Christ died for our sins according to the scriptures" (1 Corinthians 15:3). In summary fashion, the issue of sin is addressed, but what about the problem of suffering? The writers of Scripture argue that the resurrection of Jesus from the dead addresses the problem of suffering. When the righteous are resurrected in the last day, John affirms that God, "will wipe away every tear from their eyes, and death shall be no more, neither shall there be mourning nor crying nor pain anymore, for the former things have passed away" (Revelation 21:4).

The problems introduced in the beginning of the narrative (Genesis)—the problem of death and corruption—are resolved at the end of the Story by means of the resurrection, that is, our resurrection from the dead.

ORIGINS

Now, let's take a look at how a familiarity with the Story assists us in addressing some of the issues surrounding the subject of origins. A shop owner I am acquainted with introduced me to a friend of hers. The shop owner's friend happened to be a professor at the University of Riverside, California. While we were shaking hands, the shop owner informed the professor that I was a preacher. The professor was taken back a bit— much like you might expect someone to respond if they were being introduced to a vampire.

The professor regained his composure, took a friendly posture, and began informing me that when he was younger, he attended an evangelical church until he went to college and studied biology. He got a little carried away with his passionate tirade against the Bible, and championing the power of modern day science to provide man with "real" answers. He caught himself and apologized. He seemed genuinely embarrassed. He asked me if I was offended. I told him I was not.

He asked me what my thoughts on the creation/evolution debate were. I told him I would not want to begin a discussion with the controversy, but rather with rehearsing the Story of the Bible.

Here is my proposed strategy. First, tell the entire Story unapologetically. Do not tweak it or deconstruct it. In so doing, we get to tell the end of the Story which brings the narrative full circle. The end of the Story tells us we regain what was lost in the beginning. It makes sense of the beginning in the same way the beginning makes sense of the end. Each places the other in perspective. I am convinced that some might be so overwhelmed with the beauty and sublimity of the Story as a whole that the issues we sometimes get stuck on, will pale in significance.

Do not misunderstand me. I am not advocating sacrificing truth for beauty or sublimity. The issues surrounding the beginning are important: creation versus evolution; the days of creation; theistic evolution versus progressive creationism versus biblical creationism. I have drawn my own conclusions about them all. But if I may suggest, let's put first things first. What harm would it do to simply ask someone like the professor if we can first tell him the Story? He seemed like a nice enough person. If he had had the time, I think he would have said yes.

My opinion is, if we can find people who will allow us to outline the whole Story, it will help to make sense of all its parts—creation included. Even if a person struggles with questions concerning the beginning in contrast with what they believe science affirms, the impact of God being the Creator, Ruler and Redeemer of all creation, will not be lost.

THE OLD TESTAMENT

When I was young and ignorant, I used to argue that the church should not bother with the Old Testament. After all, it is called "Old," and "old is mold," isn't it? Truth be told, I was such a poor reader that this was simply an excuse to eliminate three-quarters of the entire Bible. But when you consider the entire Bible from the vantage point of the Story being told, starting in Genesis and ending in Revelation, the Old Testament contains the first three acts (as they have been outlined in this book).

Who among us would ever suggest that we should begin reading any one of Shakespeare's plays in Act 4? Why, then, should we recommend only reading the last 3 Acts of the Bible?

Here is another way to look at it. When I was young, my parents bought me a stereo record player for Christmas. In those days, that was high tech. When we played the demo record that came with the player, we were treated to its distinct stereo feature. When we spread the speakers apart, and set the needle on the record, we would hear the word " You" out of the left speaker, the word "ain't" from the right speaker, "heard" from the left speaker, "nothing" from the right speaker, and "yet" from the left speaker. "You …ain't …heard …nothing …yet," bouncing from left to right. Imagine turning one speaker off. All we would have heard are the words "You… heard… yet," or "ain't…nothing…"

Reading the Bible is like listening to stereo music. Through one speaker we hear emphasized the "Testament" or "Covenant" aspect of it. We have been very good at distinguishing between the Testaments. But I think we may have had the other speaker turned down or off—the other speaker being the story or narrative dimension of the Bible. Both speakers need to be heard in balance. Emphasizing the "Testament" dimension to the exclusions of the story dimension, perhaps we have failed to see the value of studying the Old or First Testament.

My precaution, of course, is that we do not emphasize the story or narrative dimension to such an extent that we fail to distinguish between the Covenants. My point is that turning the narrative speaker on, we will hear the practical value of studying the Old Testament. We will learn to see the continuity between the two as well as the discontinuity that exists between the two Testaments.

WORLDVIEW

Studying the Bible from beginning to end, keeping the narrative dimension before us, helps answer fundamental questions asked about the biblical worldview. When considering any worldview, we seek answers to questions like "Where are we?" "Who are we?" "What went wrong?" and "What is the solution?"

Christopher Wright, in his book, *The Mission of God*, suggests the following answers (Wright, Christopher 55, 2006):

"Where are we?" Answer: We inhabit the earth, which is part of the good creation of the one living, personal God, YHWH.

"Who are we?" What is the essential nature of humanity? We are made by YHWH in God's own image, one of God's creatures, but unique among them in spiritual and moral relationships and responsibility.

"What's wrong?" Why is the world in such a mess? Through rebellion and disobedience against our Creator God, we have generated the mess that we now see around us at every level of our lives, relationships and environment.

"What is the solution?" What can we do about it? Nothing in our selves. But the solution has been initiated by God through his choice and creation of a people, Israel, through whom God intends eventually to bring blessing to all nations of the earth and ultimately to renew the whole creation.

We all have a worldview, a basic set of beliefs through which we look at the world. Worldviews are so basic to life, that we usually don't think about them. But we think about everything else through them. The significance of a worldview can be illustrated by imagining how different our perceptions of life would be if we took the atheist's or agnostic's posture concerning the existence of God rather than the biblical view of God. Do you suppose your life would be any different if lived as an atheist? Mortimer Adler writes,

> More consequences for thought and action follow from the affirmation or denial of God than from answering any other basic question. They follow for those who regard the question as answerable only by faith or only by reason, and even for those who insist upon suspending judgment entirely (Adler 391, 1986).

ATONEMENT

As one writer put it, God did not leave us a theory on atonement. He left us a meal. The just shall not live by one theory of atonement or another, but by faith in God, and in what He did through His Son on the cross. N. T. Wright observes,

> The first thing to say is that theories of atonement are all, in themselves, abstractions from the real events. The events—the flesh-and-blood, time-and-space happenings—are the reality which the theories are trying to understand but cannot replace. In fact, the stories are closer to the events than the theories, since it is through the narratives that we are brought in touch with the events, which are the real thing, the thing that matters. And it is through other events in the present time that we are brought still closer: both the Eucharist, which repeats the meal Jesus gave as his own interpretation of his death, and the actions of healing, love and forgiveness through which Jesus' death becomes a fresh reality within the still broken world. (Wright, N. T. 94-95, 2006).

THE MISSION OF GOD

The Bible tells us about God, and about man's condition before his Creator. It tells us about God's plan to redeem mankind. Man's redemption is a major part in God's mission.

Our understanding of God comes primarily by means of God's actions as Creator, Ruler, and Redeemer, as explicated in the narrative of Scripture, rather than by abstract theories or systematic theologies. God's actions are recorded in the Bible fundamentally through the narrative.

I am not suggesting that other portions of the Bible, like the poetry, or prophets or epistles, are not of value. All Scripture is profitable (2 Tim. 3:16). Poetry reflects on God and his works in a different way—through images which are the primary building blocks of poetry. The prophets and epistles expound on the narrative portions or implicitly rely on them at almost every turn. The church's sense of mission in life should take its cue from God's mission.

> The authority for our mission flows from the Bible because the Bible reveals the reality on which our mission is based (Wright, Christopher J. H., 2006, p. 54).

Some presentations of the gospel are more abstract than concrete because they rely heavily on theories of atonement rather than on the Story on which it is all based. When our preaching is primarily focused on justification and justice, we don't need the Story. We don't even need the Old Testament for that matter. I have even seen this done in a 20 minute Bible study in which the only point made and defended was the necessity of baptism. Jesus was not preached at all. It was not very effective even though facts from the Bible were presented.

But when we preach the narrative of the gospel—the death, burial, resurrection and appearance of Christ (1 Corinthians 15)—salvation follows. Peter preached Jesus on the day of Pentecost. He preached the gospel, which consisted of Jesus being a man "attested" by God with "might works and wonders and signs that God did through Him": His crucifixion (2:23), His resurrection (v 24), His exaltation (v 33). Peter concludes, "Let all the house of Israel therefore know for certain that God has made him both Lord and Christ, this Jesus whom you crucified" (v 36). The audience cried out, "Brothers, what shall we do?" (2:36). Peter said, "Repent and be baptized every one of you in the name of Jesus Christ for the forgiveness of your sins, and you will receive the gift of the Holy Spirit" (2:38). As one brother put it, verse 36 comes before verse 38.

Acts 8:35 says of Philip,

> he opened his mouth, and beginning with this Scripture he told him the good news about Jesus. And as they were going along the road they came to some water, and the eunuch said, 'See, here is water! What prevents me from being baptized' and he commanded the chariot to stop, and they both went down into the water, Philip and the eunuch, and he baptized him. And when they came up out of the water, the Spirit of the Lord carried Philip away, and the eunuch saw him no more, and went on his way rejoicing.

Notice, Philip told the eunuch, "the good news about Jesus." In the very next verse, the eunuch said, "See, here is water! What prevents me from being baptized." Baptism is the means by which people enter the kingdom of God where Jesus reigns as King of kings and Lord of lords. (See also Gal. 3:26, 27.)

When you preach the narrative, the gospel as it centers on the story of Jesus, you also get salvation.

CONCLUDING REMARKS

Much more could be said. Perhaps other benefits come to your mind. I am simply wanting to give you a feel for the value of knowing the story or narrative dimension of Scripture. The Story plays a major unifying factor in the 66 books that make up the Bible. God is the unifying character. He reestablishes Himself as King, and builds His kingdom. Through the cross He reveals the answer to man's problem, which is the story's unifying theme.

My goal is to get you to study your Bible in light of the Story it tells.

WORKS CITED

Adams, Hazard and Leroy Searle, *Critical Theory Since Plato*, Third Edition, "On the Sublime," by Pseudo-Longinus (Boston, Massachusetts, 2005).

Adler, Mortimer. J., *The Great Books of the Western World*, Vol. 2 (Chicago, 1986).

Allen, Leonard and Danny Gray Swick, *Participating in God's Life* (Orange, California, 2001).

Bales, James D., *The Hub of the Bible – or – Acts Two Analyzed* (Shreveport, Louisiana).

Bartholomew, Craig G. and Michael W. Goheen, *The Drama of Scripture: Finding Our place in the Biblical Story* (Grand Rapids, Michigan, 2004).

Cahill, Thomas, *The Gift of the Jews: How a Tribe of Desert Nomads Changed the Way Everyone Thinks and Feels* (New York: New York, 1998).

Freeman, Hobart, *An Introduction to the Old Testament Prophets* (Chicago, IL, 1978).

Gilkey, Langdon, *Maker of Heaven and Earth: A Study of the Christian Doctrine of Creation* (Garden City, New York, 1959).

Goldingay, John, *Genesis for Everyone,* Part 1 (Louisville, Kentucky, 2010).

Kreeft, Peter, *Love Is Stronger Than Death*, (San Francisco,

California, 1979).

Lewis, C. S., *Essay Collection: Faith, Christianity and the Church* (Hammersmith, London, 2000).

——, *Mere Christianity* (New York: NY, 2001).

McKnight, Scot, *The King Jesus Gospel: The Original Good News Revisited* (Grand Rapids, MI, 2011).

Oster, Richard E, *The College Press NIV Commentary: 1 Corinthians* (Joplin, MO, 1995).

Peterson, Eugene, *Christ Plays in a Thousand Places* (Grand Rapids, MI, 2005).

Piper, John, *The Pleasure of God* (Portland, Oregon, 1991).

Ryken, Leland, *Words of Delight* (Grand Rapids, Michigan, 1992).

Ryken, Leland, James C. Wilhoit, and Tremper Longman III, *Dictionary of Biblical Imagery* (Downers Grove, Il, 1998).

Wright, Christopher J. H., *The Mission of God: Unlocking the Bible's Grand Narrative* (Downer Groves, IL, 2006).

Wright, N. T., *The Challenge of Jesus* (Downer Groves, IL, 1999).

——, *The New Testament and the People of God* (Minneapolis, MN, 1992).

16080807R00088

Made in the USA
San Bernardino, CA
18 October 2014